S0-ABY-839

CAST PEWTER JEWELRY

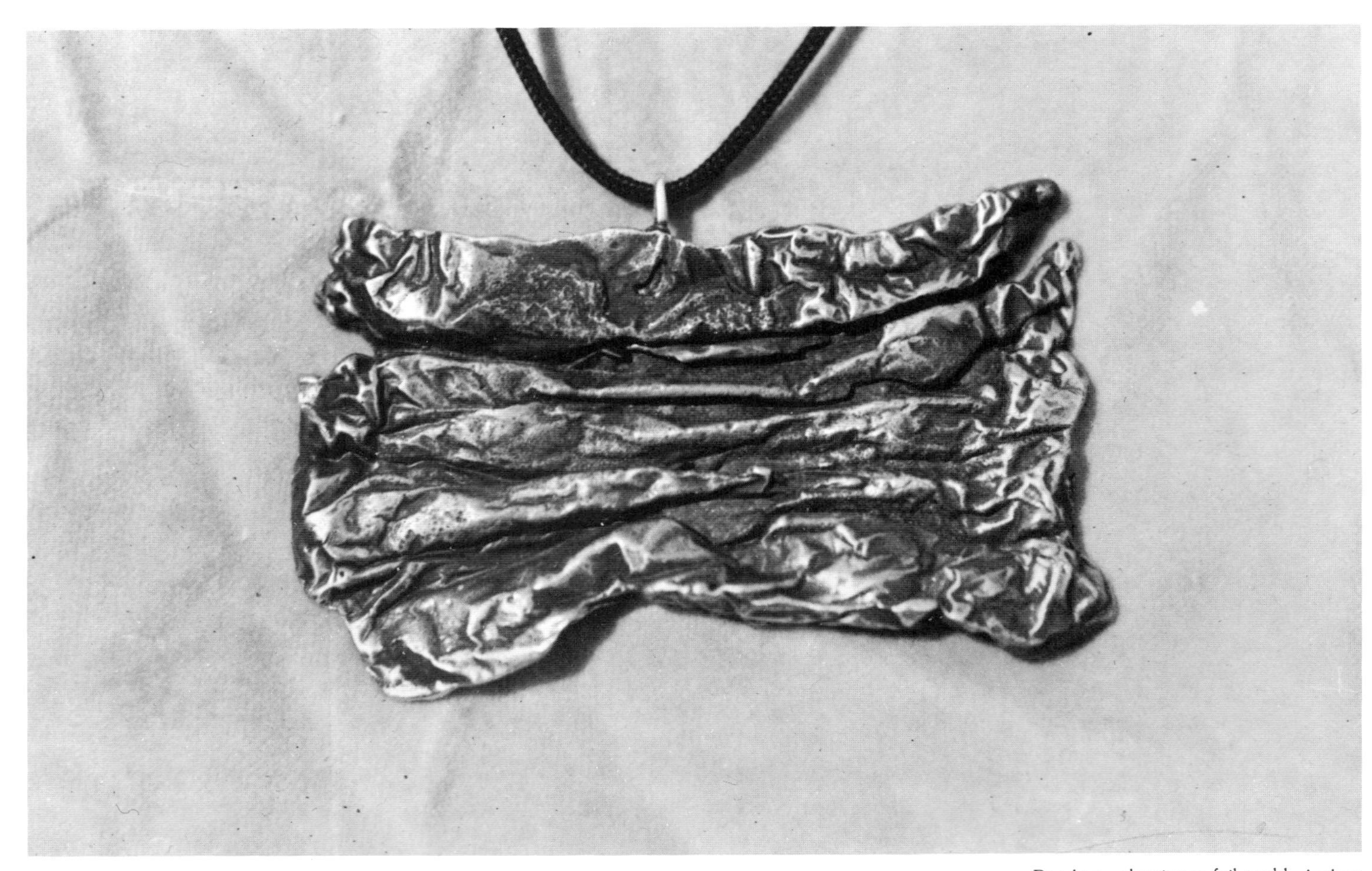

Pendant, aluminum foil mold. Author.

CAST PEWTER JEWELRY

JAY D. KAIN

Chairman, Art Department
Mansfield State College
Mansfield, Pennsylvania

DAVIS PUBLICATIONS INC. Worcester, Massachusetts

Davis Publications, Inc.
Worcester, Massachusetts, U.S.A.

Printed in the United States of America
Library of Congress Catalog Card Number: 75-10493
ISBN 0-87192-071-9

Printing: Davis Press
Type: Tiffany & Souvenir
Graphic Design by: Repro-Art Service

Consulting Editors: George F. Horn, Sarita R. Rainey

10 9 8 7 6 5 4 3 2 1

CONTENTS

ACKNOWLEDGMENTS

A special thanks to Jeanie, my wife, for her continued encouragement and artistic contributions to this endeavor. My appreciation to all my former students at the University of Minnesota and Mansfield State College for their work with pewter casting which helped to make this book possible.

INTRODUCTION

The author believes that a casting experience in pewter offers a versatile, inventive material with which to work and a "eureka" quality which the traditional metals lack, not to mention its low cost and practicality for classroom use.

This book should serve only as an impetus for the artist, student, and teacher, encouraging them to search and investigate the possibilities of pewter casting. The basic casting procedures are discussed with possible variations for each technique. A list of basic materials and equipment is included to assist in setting up a casting program in the classroom. The pewter supplied by the suggested art supply sources has no lead content.

Pendant with faceted glass, vaporization. Student.

Pendant and pin, vaporization casting. Student.

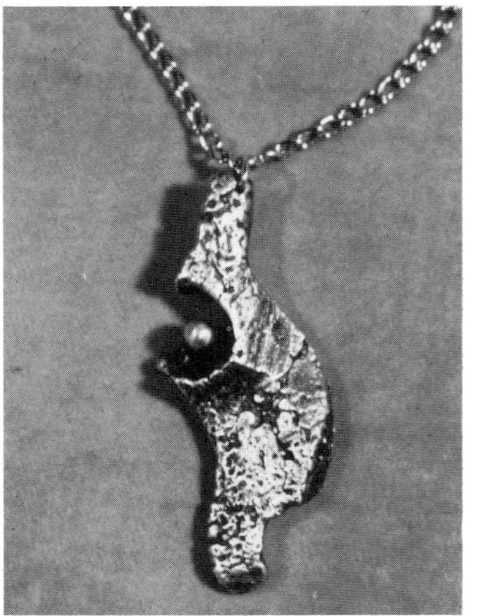

Pendant, vaporization. Student.

PEWTER I

Historically, pewter has enjoyed a long existence in man's world, but has held few places of distinction in comparison with the precious metals of gold and silver. During the Bronze Age, pewter must have been used, since both pewter and bronze are alloys of tin and copper. Because of pewter's soft and pliable nature it was not utilitarian enough to be used for tools or weapons.

Although pewter was used extensively in the Orient and throughout the Roman Empire in both ornamental and functional objects, it was not until Europe began to emerge from the Dark Ages that pewter and the pewter craft re-emerged.

The golden years of pewter in America ranged from the 1700's to about 1850. During this period colonial craftsmen followed the British tradition of working pewter. The everyday kitchen utensils or containers were the primary products produced. Early production techniques of forming pewter included casting, raising or forming by hammering into molds, spinning and shaving. With the coming of the Industrial Revolution mechanical means of turning pewter on lathes made pewter articles more available to the consumer. Today, most pewter articles are commercially cast, stamped or spun for quantity production.

Pewter usage in America today is primarily devoted to reproducing articles of the colonial period. With the exception of the Scandanavians, modern artists do not use pewter to any extent.

The alloy of pewter has consisted of many different formulae since its discovery. The primary component is always tin and is combined with other metals to produce the desired specification for the particular use. Many believe the finest pewter is an alloy of 80% tin and 20% copper. Variations of this alloy consist of different percentages of copper, antimony and bismuth which all add strength, or harden and temper the basic metal of tin. Because of the possible toxic qualities of lead it is not included in the production of pewter in America today. Silver is sometimes added to the pewter alloy but it is too soft to have an appreciable effect on the hardness of the metal.

Pewter may be acquired from numerous supply sources in either casting ingots or sheets. (See appendix for sources for lead-free pewter.) Another source for pewter is often found in the local scrap metal or junk yards. The surface of this pewter will have oxidized and collected foreign matter. Slag or impurities during the melting process will form and will have to be skimmed off the top of the molten pewter.

Following is a chart of some of the pewter formulae that have been used in the production of pewter ware by craftsmen in Europe, England and America.

Parts of . . .	Tin	Copper	Lead*	Antimony
Fine Pewter	112	26		
Plate Pewter	100	4		8
Ley Metal	80		20*	
Organ Pipe metal	60		40*	
Queen's metal	100	4		8
Britannia metal	150	3		10
or	91	2		9
or	88	2		8 brass 2
or	92			8

Britannia is also called Soft, Prince and White metal by various sources.

*The use of lead should not be included in the pewter alloy because of the possible toxic effects.

The content of the pewter alloy in the scrap articles may be determined by snapping your finger against the edge of the piece to produce a ringing sound. Caution should be used to select scrap metal that does not have a lead component. Pewter with a lead content produces a dull sound and the surface has a dull gray appearance. As pewter is soft and pliable, the surface may be scratched or bent to help identify it from other scrap metals. If there is a high content of tin in the alloy, a crackling sound will occur when the article is bent.

A third way of acquiring pewter for casting is to investigate the feasibility of alloying your own metal, if facilities are available. Local foundries or scrap metal dealers may also have the necessary equipment and facilities for alloying pewter in quantity at reasonable cost.

The maximum lead content allowed in American pewter is .05 as listed in the Annual Book of ASTM Standards.

RIGID MOLDS

Plaster Block

The technique of casting pewter utilizing plaster blocks as molds offers a fast, easy and productive means of creating jewelry objects. The inexpensive materials and supplies necessary for this process are easily acquired locally.

Casting pewter with two blocks involves the process of carving the design cavity into one block and carving a sprue opening in the other block. The two blocks are secured together so that the tip of the sprue funnel connects with the carved cavity of the design. Molten pewter is charged by gravity into the two-piece mold, filling the cavity and producing the exact form in metal.

The following list suggests supplies and equipment needed for this casting technique:

Supplies and Equipment Plaster Block

Plaster block—Approximately 3" x 4" x ¾". Must be flat on the carving side of blocks. Make your own blocks as illustrated. Allow ½ inch between design and edge of block.

Ladle—Iron skimmer ladle is the best (plumbing supply) but copper, clay or old soup ladles (dipper) will work. Should have handle to protect from heat.

Pewter—Ingots, scrap or sheet pewter may be melted. Melts at approximately 450-500°F.

Wire—Stove pipe, copper wire or C-clamps to secure the molds together for casting. The use of flammable materials should be avoided.

Carving Tools—Any rigid tool that will carve, scratch or dig into the plaster will work, such as, knife, linoleum carving tools, nails, pieces of metal, wooden sticks, sharp stones and pencils.

Torch—Propane torch (TX-9 tank) produces sufficient heat to melt pewter. Gas stoves and electric hot plates can also serve as a substitute heat source.

Other supplies—Brushes for cleaning carved cavity. Abrasive paper for flattening blocks if necessary. Casting pit-container with sand or dirt. Steel wool, hand buff, tripoli and rouge for polishing. Nitric acid for oxidizing pewter, 1 part acid into 5 parts water. ACID INTO WATER. Glass container, and tongs, plastic or copper. Additives—beads, wire, feathers, stones, sticks, pearls. Findings—cord, chains, pin backs, etc.

Motivation for jewelry designs and ideas exists in numerous places. Possible sources would include discarded articles and objects from nature. It is suggested that you keep these in a "design box", an accessible source for ideas. Seeking patterns and textures in nature objects will help to excite the imagination with possible surface textures and designs for jewelry. Looking through a microscope will open new worlds and stimulate new thought for shapes, lines, patterns and colors that may be translated into jewelry structures. Making an aperture from a piece of paper with a cut-out square will help the artist to see repetitions and new formations in grass, clover and other small surfaces and areas that might otherwise go unnoticed.

Man-made objects are excellent sources for textures, patterns, surfaces, contrasts or designs that could be incorporated into jewelry ideas. The interesting and varied structures of radiator grills of diesel trucks, stacks of concrete drain pipes, patterns of cracks in sidewalks and walls, designs on old door knobs and gears are but a few of the possible sources of motivation for designs. Original jewelry designs are rewarding experiences and offer countless opportunities for personal expression.

Clamp the wood frame to the masonite base and seal the joints with clay. Brush a solution of soap and water onto the surface to help release the plaster blocks. Mix the molding plaster in a bucket to a heavy cream consistency and pour into a large mold. Tap the table to remove the air bubbles.

After the plaster sets up (20-30 minutes), inscribe lines for the desired size of blocks needed. Remove frame and flex the masonite back to release sections of the plaster blocks. Break individual blocks into desired size.

Containers stacked in modular formation offer provocative ideas for surface textures on metal jewelry.

Man's cultivation and occupation of the earth might stimulate thoughts of patterns and forms for jewelry design.

The linear markings or striations of the surface of a tree could be interpreted into grooved surface areas in metal.

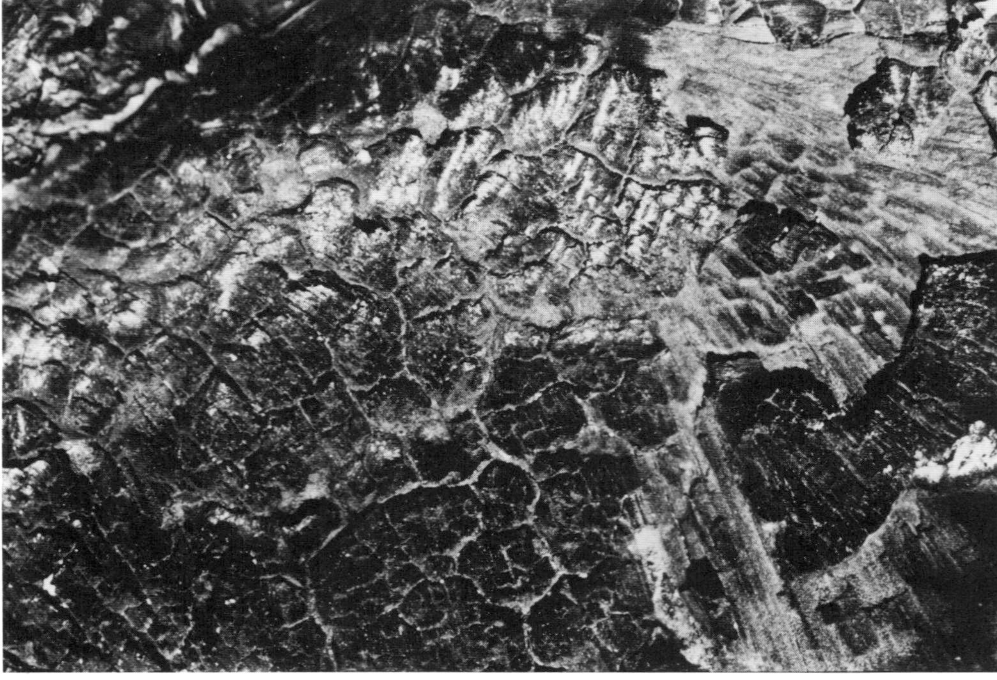

Nature provides an abundance of lines, textures, surfaces, shapes and forms to discover and investigate for the observant eye.

Structures, constructions, junk, fences, facades, manhole covers, walls are a part of our environment providing new images and discoveries and encouraging sensitivity.

A free transfer often adds, modifies and enhances the design quality as well as introduces one to the carving material. Working directly in the plaster block with the carving tools, without a sketch or design, is still another rewarding experience to the neophite and experienced craftsman alike.

Plaster blocks normally require three to seven days to sufficiently air dry before they can be charged with molten pewter. Forced drying, placing the blocks in a warm oven, using an infrared heat lamp or placing them in the direct sun light, will hasten the process. Carving and working the mold may start as soon as the plaster has set up for about an hour. Moist plaster is much easier to carve, but difficulty may be encountered in smoothing the carved surface. Plaster blocks which are completely dry and void of moisture may be sponged with water to facilitate carving the design in the mold. Newspaper spread around the working area will aid in cleaning.

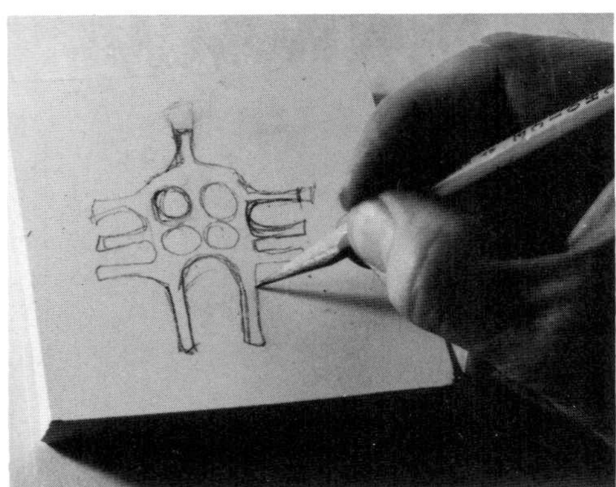

Once the design is selected, transfer it to the block in one of several different ways: sketch the design directly onto the smooth side of the block, or

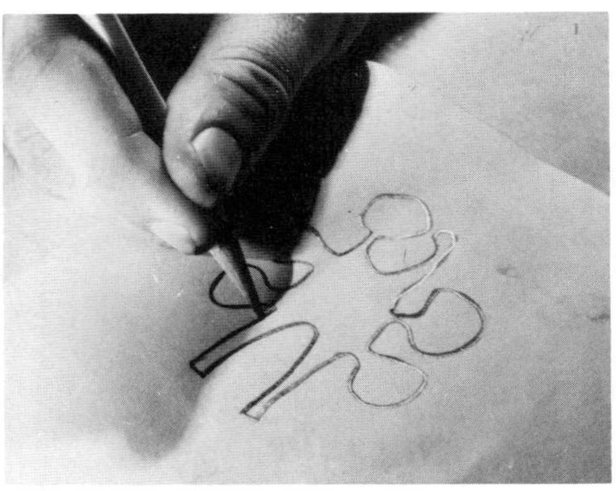

Trace the design from drawing paper onto the block; the casting will be the reverse of the drawing.

Rub graphite onto the back of the paper which makes an excellent "carbon paper" for transferring to the block.

Place pencil drawing face down onto the block and burnish the back of the paper which will transfer the line drawing to the block.

The casting from this transfer technique will be exactly the same as the original drawing.

Jewelry designs with filigree or open area structures are developed by carving channels into the flat surface of the mold, leaving plaster between the cuts. A channel cut in a circle, leaving the flat surface of the block in the center, will cast as a ring of metal. The depth of the channels depends on the amount of filigree and the size of the carved design. The cuts should be of sufficient depth to allow the molten metal to flow to all parts of the cavity. Take a test casting to determine if the metal will flow properly to all areas.

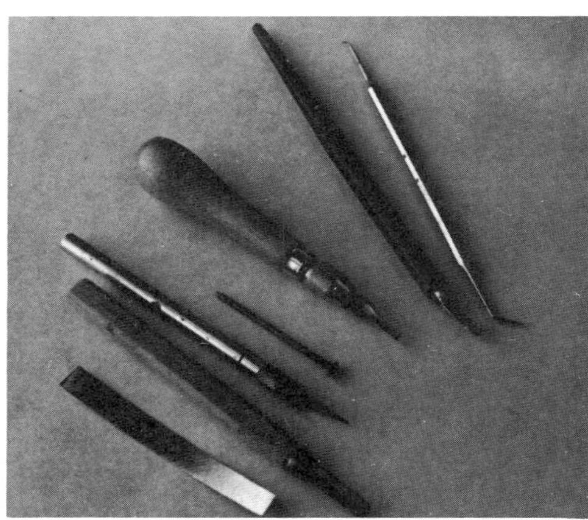

Use a stencil knife, nails, linoleum carving tools, old dental tools, wood carving tools or a piece of metal as utensils for carving the designs in the plaster block.

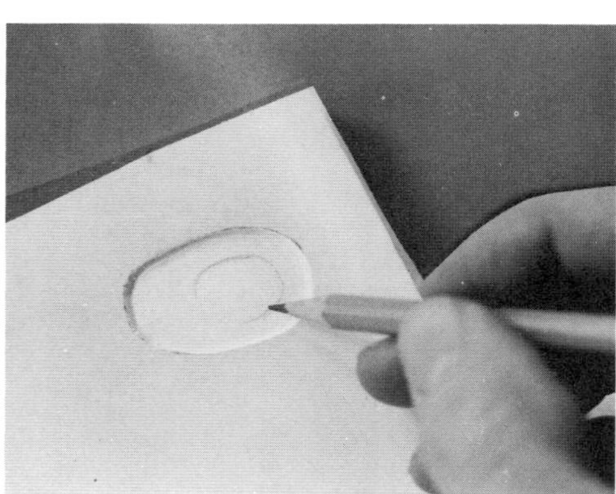

Carve the basic shape first, and then draw in the second depth.

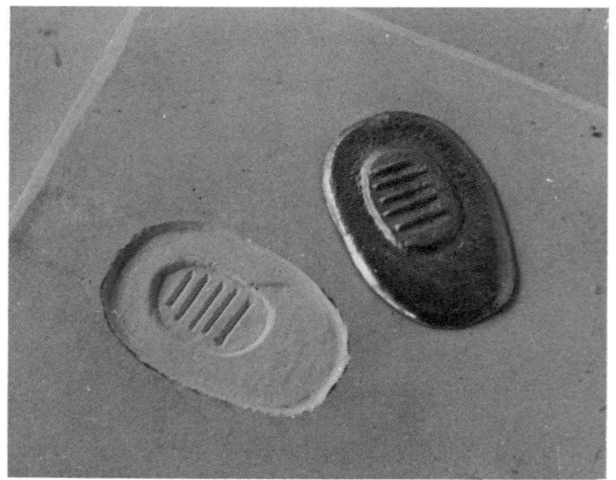

Carve the second level in the mold. This will protrude on the cast piece of jewelry. Surface decorations create the third level in the mold.

If the mold is to be used for more than one casting, as for cuff links, earrings or modular units, it is essential that "undercuts" be avoided. Undercut areas that have been carved back under the surface edge of the design prohibits the release of the casting. The mold should be carved so the metal, when cast in the cavity, will lift away or release from the mold without breaking or destroying the plaster walls. Undercuts may be desired for particular shapes or forms, but the mold may only be used once.

A wire is drilled into the plaster block before casting to post a pearl or set a stone after the piece has been cast. This post will remain in the mold during casting.

Hold the two blocks together with a C-clamp and place the secured mold in a casting pit. Sand or dirt in an old can or pie pan will prevent the molten metal from spilling.

One of the unique qualities of casting pewter with the two piece plaster mold is the lack of heat damage to the mold during the casting process. This enables the artist to make test casting for judging and identifying the design quality and function of the piece. If the test casting isn't satisfactory the artist can continue to carve the design or create a progressive series of pieces from the same mold.

Heat metal with a torch or on a stove and, when completely molten, charge directly into sprue opening until filled.

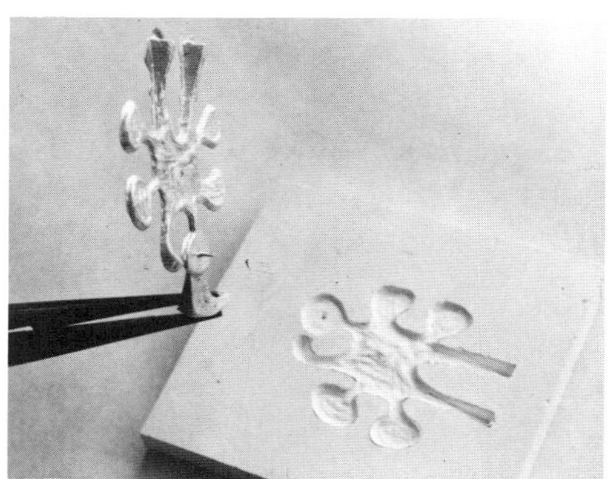

Remove the wire or clamp and lift off the sprue block cautiously, carefully lifting the casting from the mold with pliers. Finish the cast piece as suggested in Chapter IV and then glue the pearl or stone on its post.

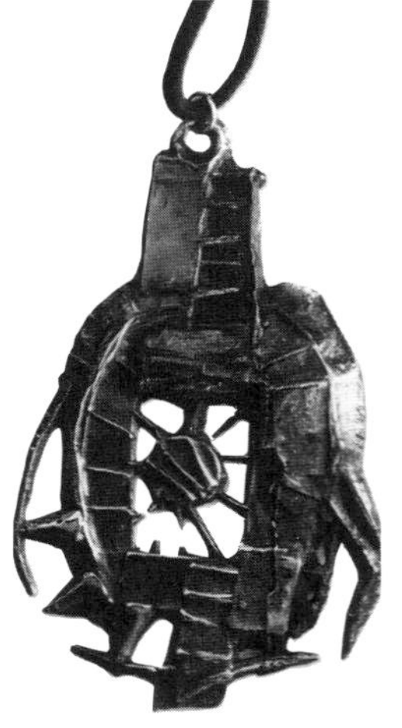

Pendant from a plaster block casting. Student.

Setting a cabochon stone with a metal bezel may be accomplished by carving a V-shaped channel in the plaster mold around the placement of the object. It is best to carve the bezel slightly larger and deeper than the stone. This allows for shrinkage and refinement of the cast bezel. After the piece is finished and the stone placed in the mounting, a chasing tool is used to push the metal bezel securely around the stone. Pewter prongs or posts may also be cast directly on the piece by drilling tapered holes into the mold.

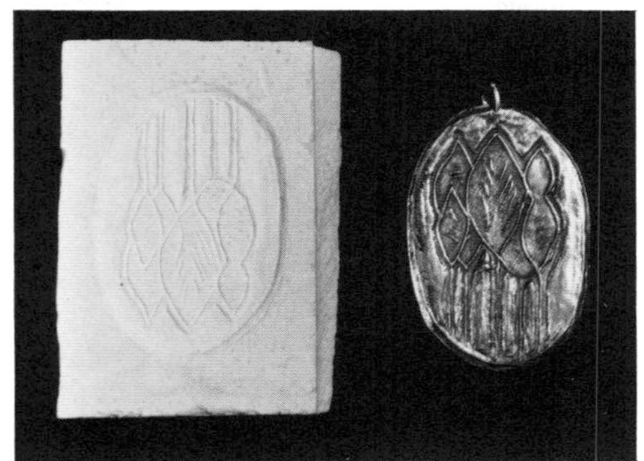

Pendant and plaster mold. Student.

Pendant. Student.

Pendant. Student.

Hair barrette, cast in plaster block and forged. Student.

Three pins, progressive casting from the same mold. Student.

Necklace from one mold. Student.

Another technique, usable with objects or materials that are not affected by the heat of the pewter, is to carve a similar impression or shape of the object in the mold and glue the stone or object in the mold. The portion of the stone that is glued will be exposed after casting, while the rest of the stone or object will be secured in pewter.

A conical-shaped sprue is carved in the wood or plaster sprue block. The block is aligned with the design so the end or tip of the sprue will overlap, approximately a quarter of an inch, into the carved cavity. The two blocks are secured together and are ready for casting. The top of the sprue should be as large as possible and should taper to a point, so the metal will flow smoothly into the mold. The large opening makes it easier to pour the molten pewter into the sprue

Cuff links. Author.

Bracelet from one mold. Student.

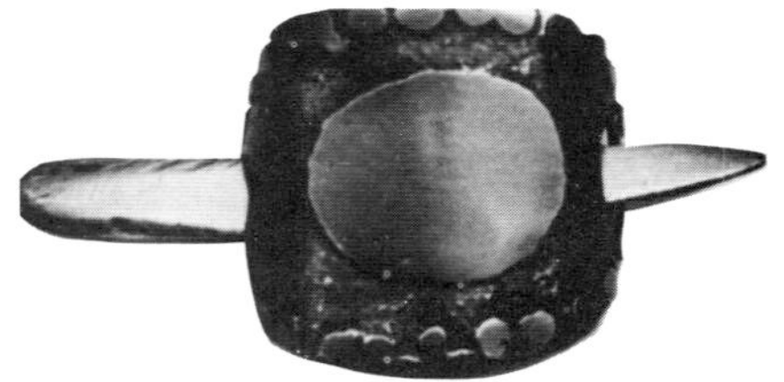

Hair barrette, cast flat in plaster mold and forged to shape. Student.

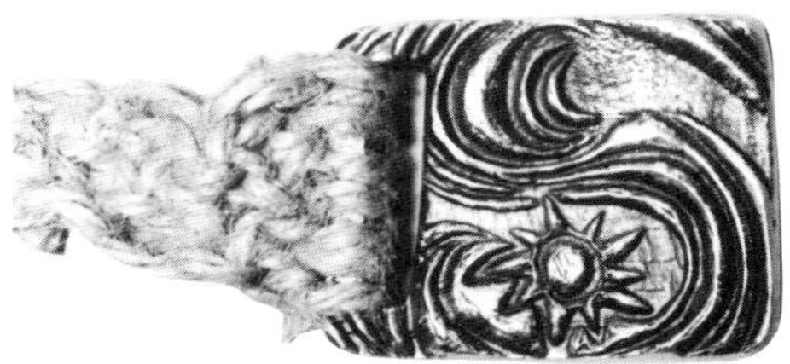
Buckle. High school student.

Buttons. Student

Pendant. Student.

On large pieces, such as belt buckles, two sprues (sprue and riser) may be used to insure that metal flows to all parts of the mold.

Sculptural effects can be achieved for pendants and other jewelry pieces by carving designs in both the front and back blocks of the mold. The two blocks are aligned, and each is then carved. After carving, the blocks are realigned to produce a three-dimensional cavity between them.

The placement of the sprue block and the carved block may be adjusted to any position that would facilitate the flow of the metal to the cavity. The sprue block may be placed in a position that would make it possible to incorporate the cast metal sprue as a functional part of the piece. Wooden sprue blocks, cut from a smooth piece of white pine, may be used and reused many times for casting. The wood is harder to carve or file than plaster but the flatness and the block's reuse makes it worth the effort.

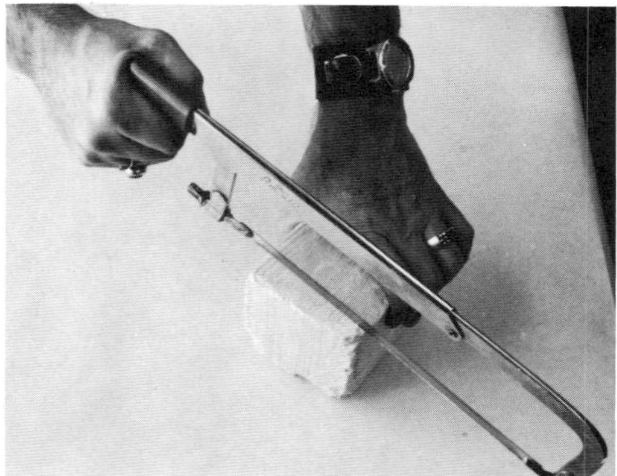

Sculpstone is an organic stone which is hard to carve but will not crumble while working.

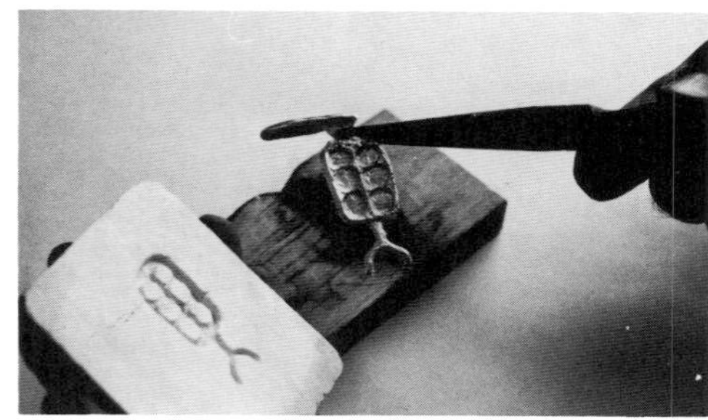

Remove the pewter casting gently to avoid damaging the mold. Delicate designs and details may be achieved in the sculpstone.

Pendant, Sculpstone mold. Student.

Cuff links, Sculpstone mold. Student.

Maple rock is a natural stone of very light composition which will reproduce minute detail. A cabochone stone glued in the impression of the mold ready for casting.

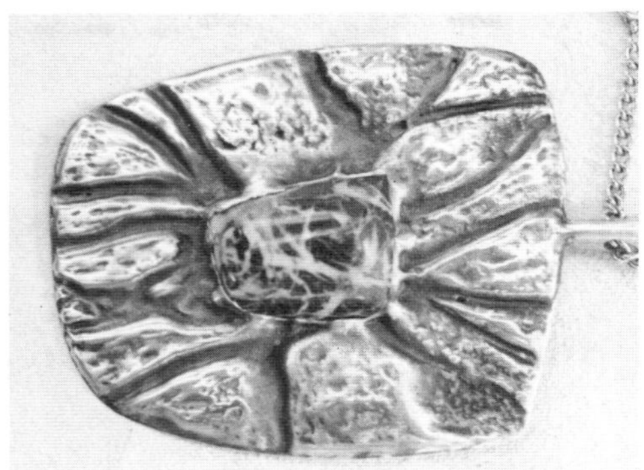

Finished piece with stone encased in pewter. Student.

Finished casting from Maple rock. Author.

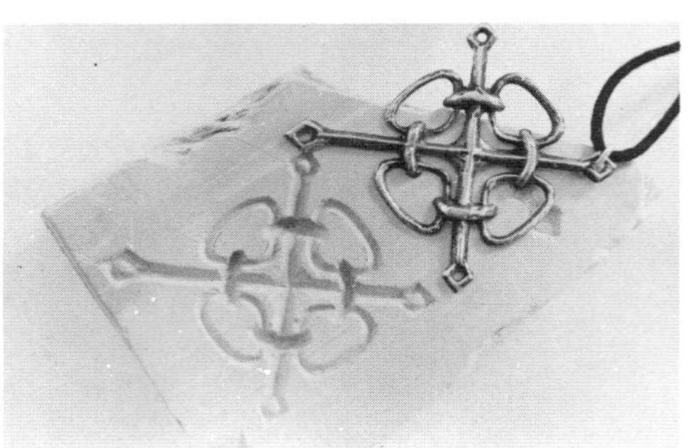

Pendant and Maple rock mold. Student.

All the moisture must be out of the plaster molds before the casting procedure may begin. If moisture is retained in the blocks, the damp mold will "spit" the molten pewter out of the sprue. Exercise caution by always wearing goggles, asbestos gloves and appropriate clothing. When the two blocks are moistureless they are placed together in the proper alignment for casting and are secured by flexible wire, C-clamps or tape. Care should be taken that the blocks don't move or slip from the desired placement. The blocks should be flush with each other. If light shows between the two blocks it is a good indication that the pewter will flow out of the mold.

After securing the mold blocks together they are placed in a container of sand (silica, ordinary play sand or even dirt), which serves as a casting pit. Pack the sand around the mold to support it in position and to restrict molten metal from flowing through any openings around the bottom or side of the mold.

Four Pendants. Student. The Sandcore molds material was acquired from local casting foundries.

Pendant with stone cast in Sandcore mold. Student.

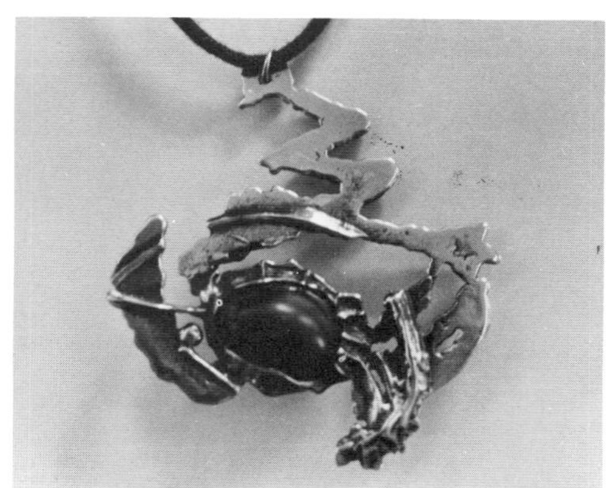

The back of the above pendant carved in a combination of Sandcore and plaster block clamped together. Student.

Many types of containers may be used to melt the pewter but the iron skimmer ladle is the best as it allows only the pure metal to flow into the mold. Since pewter melts at a relatively low temperature, a propane torch is adequate for the job. Gas stoves and even electric hot plates will heat the ladle sufficiently to melt the pewter but it takes a longer time. Small pieces of pewter are placed in the melting side and heat is applied until the entire mass is molten. A dark scum of slag or impurities will appear on the molten surface but will not affect the pewter except to act as a heat insulator from the torch. These impurities may be skimmed off or pushed to one side of the ladle with a graphite stick or an old piece of metal. Flux does not need to be added to facilitate the flowing of the pewter as is necessary with other metals.

Flat pieces of wood provide an excellent mold material for casting low melting temperature pewter. The carved design in the wood follows the grain. Rough pewter casting.

Finished pendant and pin cast from a wood mold.

Pendant. Wood mold. Student.

The clean molten pewter will flow under the gates in the bottom of the skimmer ladle to the casting side and will acquire the same level on both sides. When the metal first melts it will lay flat on the surface, similar to water. Additional heat will cause it to ball up, similar to mercury, at which point it is ready to charge into the mold (approximately 600-625°F). The torch is directed at both the lip of the ladle and at the metal as the molten pewter is charged directly into the sprue opening with a continuous flow. When the molten metal backs up and fills the sprue, the charging is completed.

Charcoal blocks have traditionally been used as molds for metals with high melting temperatures. The blocks are easy to carve, but details are hard to achieve.

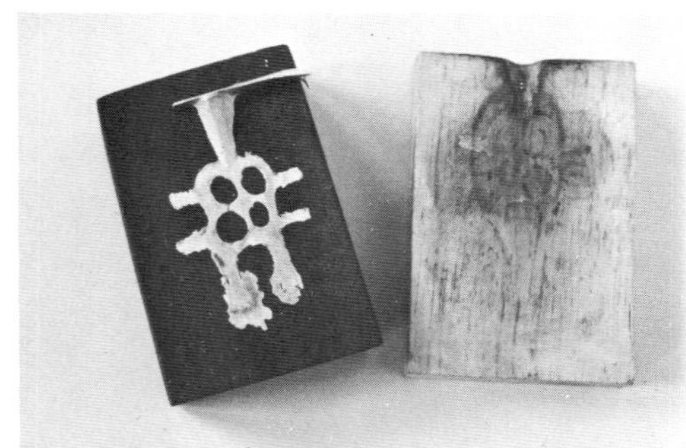

Mold and wood sprue block separated showing the back of the pewter casting.

The rough casting with the sprue and flashes of metal.

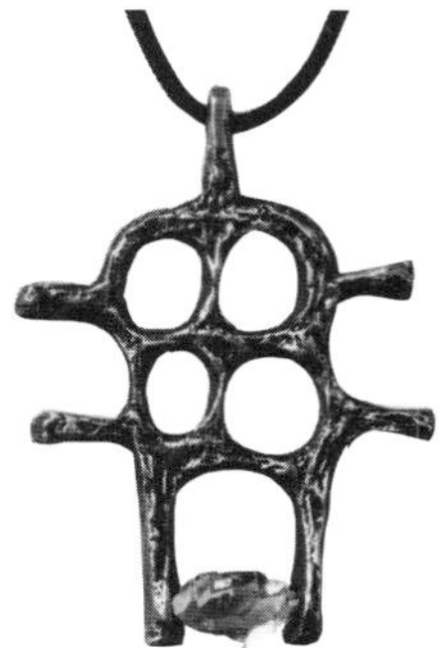

The finished pendant with a Herkimer diamond. Author.

This technique of gravity casting permits the metal to flow downward and into all cavities of the mold by the weight of the metal alone. Small air vents should be scratched in the plaster mold to relieve gas locks that might occur during charging. Accurate impressions or casting of delicate work can be achieved by this casting technique.

A variation to the previous casting technique is to place the carved block face up in the sand and pour the molten pewter directly into the carved cavity. The metal will rise above the surface level of the block as it fills the design area. This will add weight to the object and does not always give accurate impressions. To reduce the weight of this casting a back block may be pressed down on top of the molten pewter, forcing the excess out between the two blocks.

After the pewter has solidified, the two-piece mold may be removed from the casting pit and opened with caution. The C-clamps or securing devices are removed and the two pieces are held level, with the front block on the bottom. This allows the back block to be lifted away, exposing the back of the cast object. The cast piece is removed from the mold with pliers, taking care not to break the walls of the mold. Finishing of the pewter piece may follow the suggested procedure in Chapter IV.

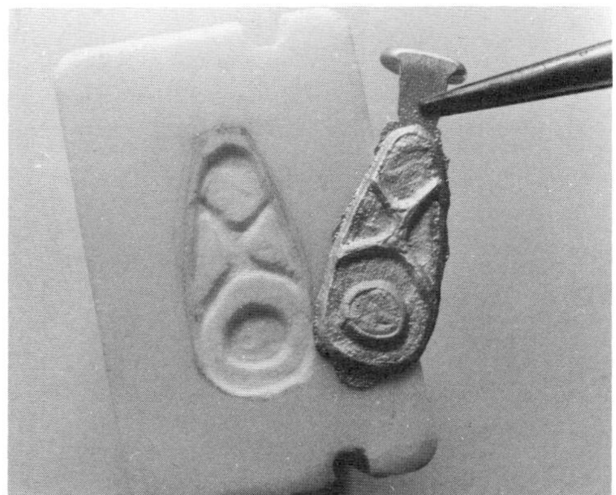

A popular sculpture material, salt blocks may also be used as mold blocks for pewter casting. Because of the hardness, it is difficult to achieve detail. Mold and rough casting.

Pendant cast from salt block. Student.

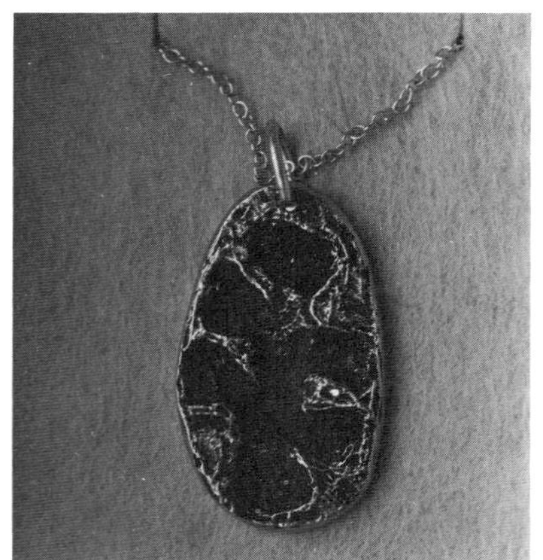

Pendant. Student.

The major advantages of using the plaster blocks as molds for casting pewter is the accessability of moulding plaster and the low cost of making them in the classroom. The smoothness of the plaster and the control over carving it facilitate the means for precise and accurate castings in metal. The durability of the plaster enables the molds to be recharged many times with the low temperature casting pewter. Many other materials or formulae for investment may be used for mold blocks which will give specific qualities to the metal casting. The examples of sculpstone, maple rock, sand-core, wood, charcoal, salt block and cuttlefish bone indicate a few of the materials that may be used to develop a two-piece mold that will accept molten pewter. The basic process of developing the carved design in the mold and the casting should follow the preceding plaster block technique.

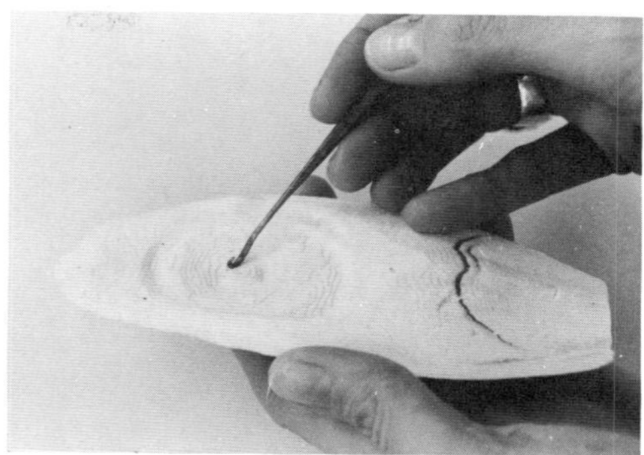

Flat surfaces can be obtained by sawing the cuttlefish bone in half or sanding one side. Designs may be scraped, cut or pressed into soft cuttlebone.

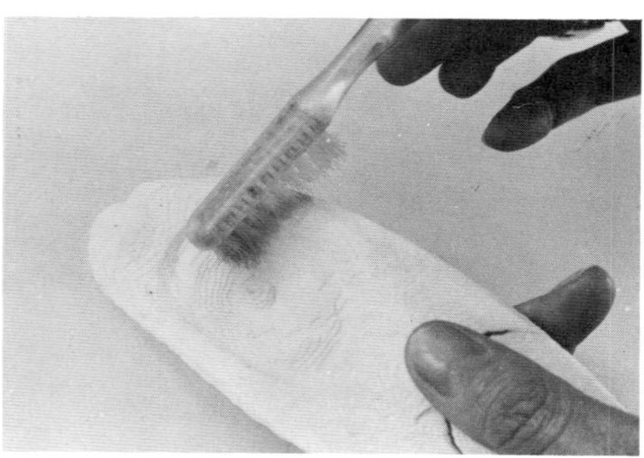

Use a toothbrush to emphasize the inherent textures of the bone. Secure a wood sprue block to the cuttlebone to prepare it for charging.

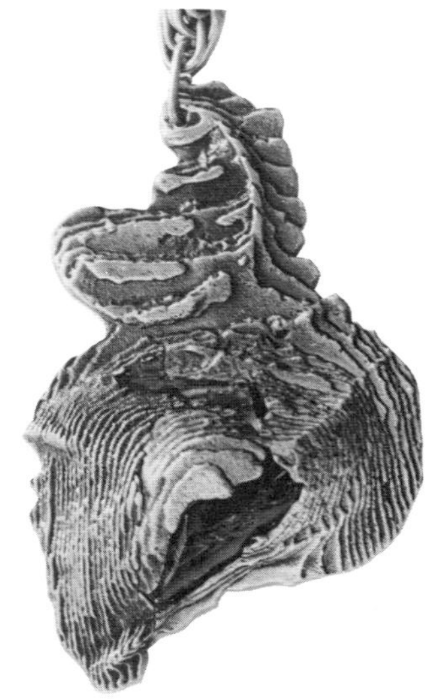

Pendant cast with stone. Texture was created by brushing cuttlebone model with toothbrush and securing stone in the mold for casting. Student.

Pendant. Brushed cuttle bone texture with impression. Student.

Pendant. Carved and brushed. Student.

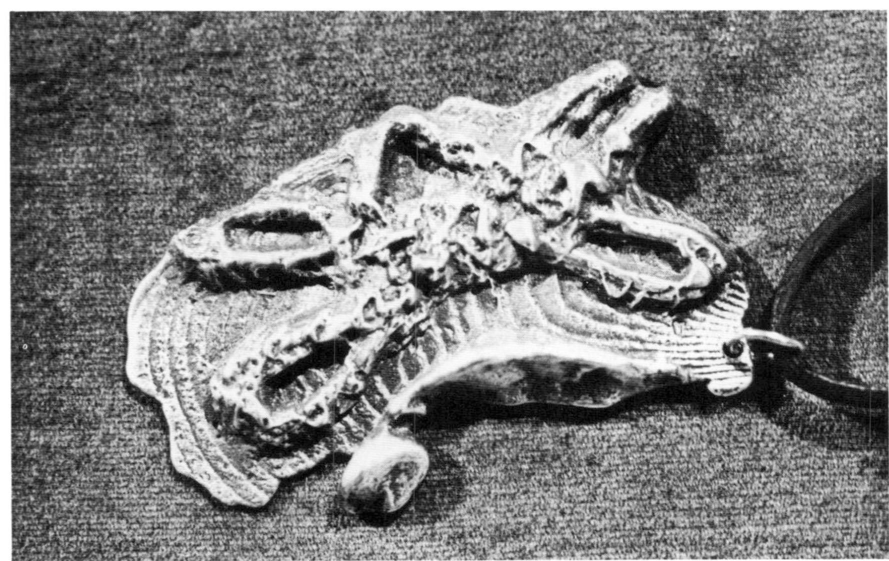

Pendant. Carved and brushed. Student.

Four pendants from one mold. Recarved after each casting.

Lost Wax in Plaster Block

In all of the techniques previously described and illustrated, the artist carves his design in reverse in the mold block. A simple technique for working in the positive form using moulding plaster is to develop an exact model in wax with a flat surface on the back. The mold is then glued to the bottom of a cardboard box. Plaster is mixed and poured beside and over the wax model, filling the box. When the plaster has set up, the paper box may be removed from the plaster and the block left to dry. Place the dried block in an old pie pan on an angle and apply heat slowly with a propane torch. The wax will melt and expose the concave mold formed in the plaster. If the mold is to be reused, care should be taken to insure that there are no undercuts in the mold cavity.

Glue the wax model in the box, face up. Pour the plaster into the box next to the wax model. Tap the table to remove any air locks or bubbles.

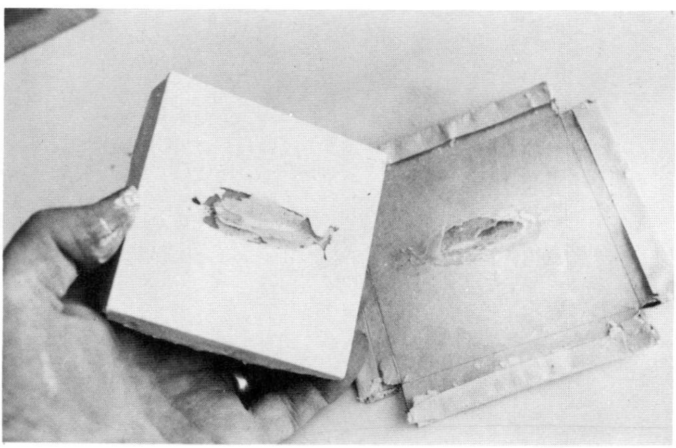

Remove the plaster block from the cardboard box to expose the back of the wax model.

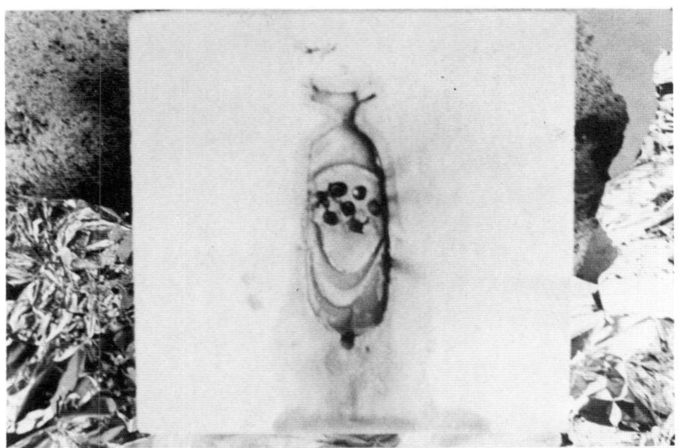

Place the block on an angle over foil or a pan and heat with a torch to melt the wax and expose the design cavity. Clean off the rough edges and the block is ready to be charged.

Finished pewter pendant.

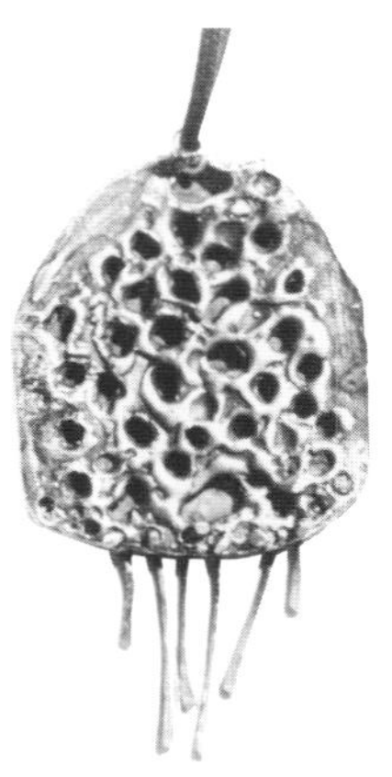

Pendant, silver wire. Student.

Three-Piece Mold

To offer more versatility in casting, a three-piece (or more) mold can be used to cast an object with more dimension. For a three-piece mold, such as a ring mold, two small wooden blocks are used with a plaster block. The plaster mold serves as the head mold of the ring. The two wood blocks have a ring shank and sprue carved in them. The wooden blocks are secured together and then aligned on the plaster to fit over the carved head and all three pieces are secured together. Care should be taken to make sure that all touching surfaces are flat. Clay or plasticene may be forced into the seams around the blocks to insure that the metal does not flow through the joints of the mold.

A three-piece plaster block with carved ring design, a carved ring shank with sprue and back block.

The ring shank and sprue blocks clamped together and secured to the plaster block ready for charging.

The finished ring with a cast ring band.

Ring with stone. The stone was secured in the design of the mold before charging.

Lost Wax

Casting pewter in the lost wax technique is similar to the casting of silver or gold except for the temperature of the mold during the charging of the metal. Succinctly, the lost wax technique requires a model made from material that will melt or burn. The model is embedded in a heat resistant investment and allowed to set-up. The flask is placed in a kiln and heat is gradually applied, causing the wax model to melt and vaporize (lost wax), leaving its impression or cavity in the investment. Into this cavity, left by the wax matrix in the investment material, molten metal may be gravity charged to produce an exact replica in metal. The following list indicates the suggested materials needed for the lost wax technique.

Waxes—

Any waxes may be used for their specific quality of workability and surface quality.

Beeswax, sculpture wax, parafin, dental wax (sheet), File-A-Wax, and wire wax, etc.

Replica — Any article that will burnout in the kiln and not leave an ash residue, i.e. bugs, pods, nut meats, etc.

Tools and equipment—

Wax working tools may be made from wire or old dental tools.

Alcohol lamp — to heat tools or wax — hot water, razor blade or X-acto knife — for cutting or shaving wax.

Brushes — to apply debubblizer and investment.

Tin cans — for metal flask, open on one or both ends.

Dowel rod — mandrel for rings, masking tape and aluminum foil.

Ladle — iron skimmer for melting pewter.

Burnout kiln — small kiln, hotplate and flower pot or torch.

Torch — propane, butane or Prestolite.

Debubblizer — surface tension reducer, may use green soap and peroxide or alcohol.

Investment — commercial (cristobalite, "satin-cast", etc.) or 200 mesh silica (3 parts) to plaster of paris (1 part).

Many varieties of waxes are available for making models for the lost wax technique.

A three-dimensional wax object with vent and sprue attached. Apply debubblizer to the wax model with a soft brush and blow off the excess with a soda straw.

A variety of waxes with specific qualities are available for the creation of various effects: Soft pliable sculpture wax may be molded by squeezing and forming with the hands; File-A-Wax may be carved with a knife or filed with a metal file to refine the shape and surface; dental base plate wax sheets may be cut out with a razor or knife and appliqued, molded, sculptured or incised and worked in many ways to develop the desired wax object for casting in metal.

Stones included in the wax model during the forming and development stages and then removed will leave an impression of the stone. After the casting is completed the stone is replaced in the impression in the metal object and secured.

After completing the wax model and obtaining the desired surface, a sprue is connected to the back of the model or to a place on the model that can be easily refined after casting. The wax sprue is made in a cone shape with the point connected to the model. Vents or wax wires should be attached to the top most part of the wax object with the other end attached to the top of the sprue. During the casting process these vents will permit gases to escape from the mold, allowing the pewter to fill the cavity and reproduce every minute detail.

Sift investment into water until a mountain appears through the water level. Mix the investment with the fingers to insure proper consistency and then pour into the tin can flask.

Push the wax model into the investment with a swirling motion to remove any air bubbles from the surface of the model.

Hold the wax model in the investment by the sprue, using the metal wires as a guide.

One technique of investing the model for pewter casting is to attach the model with the wax sprue and air vents to a paper towel with a hot wax tool. A tin can (flask) with both ends open is placed over the model and filled with investment. Another method involves filling a tin can (only one end open) with investment, placing the wax model into the flask and holding it by the sprue until the investment has set-up.

In preparing the mixture of investment, an easy means of measuring the correct amount of warm water is to place the flask on the palm of the hand and fill it until the water is ½ of an inch from the top of the tin can. Pour the water into a rubber bowl and add the investment by sifting it through the fingers until a mound of investment appears through the water. Mix the water and investment carefully with the fingers to a thin creamy consistency. Vibrate or tap the bowl to remove the bubbles in the mixture. "Setting up" time for the investment will vary with the individual mixture, but 10 to 15 minutes is normal.

After removing the wires and the wax sprue, place the flask in the cold burnout kiln. Leave the door open during the first stage of the burnout. A number of flasks may be burned out at one time.

When the burnout process is completed (all the wax is lost and the investment has turned black and then back to white again), remove the flask from the kiln and place it on asbestos or sand in the casting area. Note the sprue hole with the air vent hole at the edge. When the flask's temperature is approximately 400-500°F, charge the molten pewter with a steady flow into the sprue. Keep the torch on the lip of the ladle.

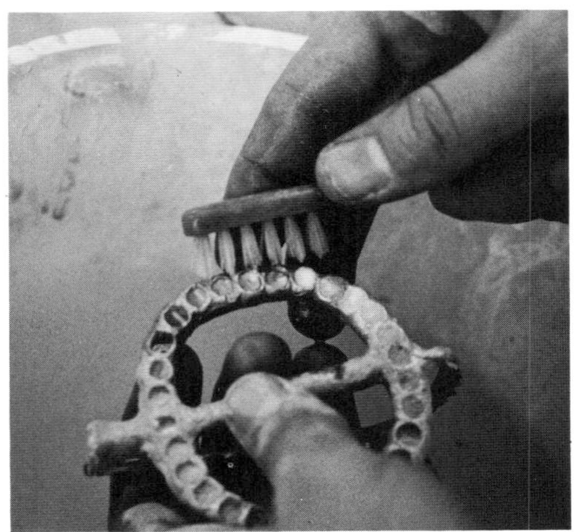

After the metal solidifies, remove the investment with the assistance of water, a knife and, finally, a toothbrush.

A soft brush may be used to flow a coat of investment over the debubblized model. The investment is then blown off and the process is repeated to insure a complete and smooth coverage. The model is swirled into the can of investment and held in place until the investment stiffens. Care should be taken that the model does not touch the sides or bottom of the flask. If the open ended flask is used the tin can is placed over the model which is secured to a paper towel by the sprue. Clay or soft wax is placed around the flask to hold it in place and to keep it sealed. Slowly pour the investment down the side of the flask or down a stick to keep air bubbles from forming. The investment is filled to the top of the masking tape secured around the flask and allowed to settle. This excess investment may be cut off after it has partially set up. The wax sprue is popped out after the investment is completely set up and the sprue hole is smoothed and rinsed out with water quickly. The flask is left to set up completely (20 to 30 minutes) before it is ready to be placed in the burnout kiln.

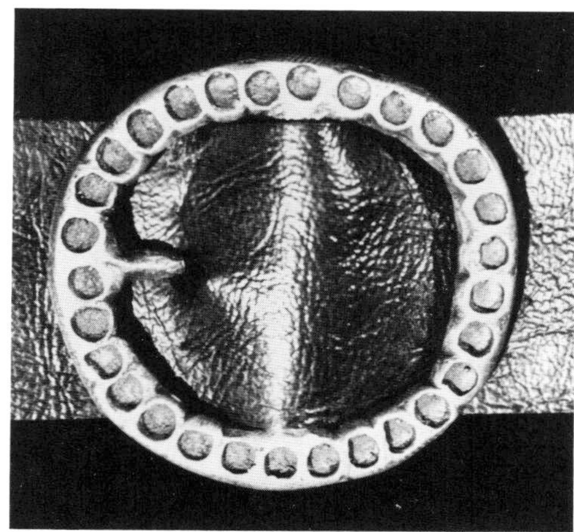

Finished buckle and belt. Student.

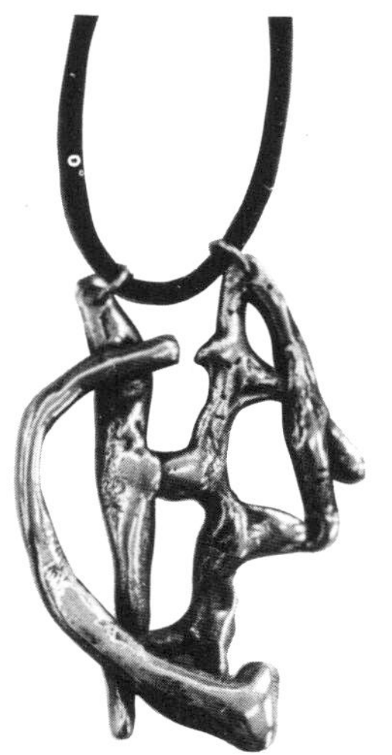

Pendant. Student.

The burnout of the flask may be accomplished in many types of kilns but a small enameling or a "burnout" type kiln works the best. A flower pot, lined with aluminum foil and placed on a hot plate, will even reach sufficient temperatures for small flasks to burn out the wax. The flasks should be placed in the cold kiln on an angle, with the sprue facing down. This position allows the wax to run out during the first stage of burnout. The temperature should be gradually increased to approximately 1100 degrees F. and maintained until the wax is completely burned out of the investment. The first stage is a critical time as the wax and/or water in the investment should not be permitted to boil because it will expand and crack the mold. The temperature of the kiln may be controlled by opening and closing the door or lid.

Cristobalite and some of the other commercial investments visually tell us when the burnout is completed. The investment starts with a white coloring, turns black as the temperature increases and then back to totally white again when the wax has burned out of the cavity and the flask is ready to be removed from the kiln. The length of time will range from 45 minutes to 3 hours, depending on the size of the flask. This stage should not be rushed as the investment will crack and break down under rapid change of temperatures.

Pendant with jade. Student.

Pendant. Student.

Safety precautions should be taken when casting by wearing goggles, gloves and long sleeves. The casting area should be free of flammable materials and only the person casting should be in the immediate area. The pewter will solidify in 5 to 10 minutes depending on the temperature of the flask. Submerge the flask in an old can filled with water, dig out the investment and clean the object with an old tooth brush. The tin can and investment should be discarded. Do not put the investment down the sink drain.

After all the investment is removed from the object, the sprue and vents are cut off with a saw and may be remelted for another casting. The finishing of the pewter piece may follow the same procedures suggested in Chapter IV.

Pendant with agate. Student.

Bracelets. Student.

FLEXIBLE MOLDS AND CASTING VARIATIONS

Vaporization or Full Mold

The relatively new casting process of foam vaporization can offer an exciting experience in casting as well as the final reward of the uniquely creative pewter jewelry. The process, from the development of the model to the finished piece of jewelry, may take as little time as 20 to 30 minutes to complete. Succinctly, the vaporization or full mold technique involves the following steps: forming the casting model from polystyrene foam; packing the foam model in a foundry or jeweler's sand in a tin can flask with a dowel rod spruce; removing the dowel rod to provide a passageway for the molten metal to reach the foam model; charging the molten pewter into the sprue funnel and directly onto the foam (the molten pewter will melt the foam and replace it in the sand mold, producing an exact pewter replica of the foam model); removing the rough pewter casting from the sand mold and cleaning the foam residue from the object; finally, finishing and polishing the cast jewelry piece as suggested in the next chapter.

The foam vaporization process requires very good ventilation in both the working and casting areas to avoid excessive exposure to fumes of the burning foam.

The following list indicates the suggested materials needed for the vaporization casting process:

Foam—

Polystyrene: open and closed cell structure, identified by the rigidness. The foam used for Christmas decoration, etc. is open cell (Styrofoam) and the foam used for packing material is mostly closed cell. Always have good ventilation when working with any foam.

DO NOT USE polyethylene or Ethofoam as the fumes from burning are extremely toxic. This foam may be identified by the flexibility of the material, such as mattresses, water skiing belts.

Dowel rod—

To be used as a sprue and funnel former, a round pencil will also work.

Tin can—

To be used as a flask for packing sand and model into. One end opened.

Sand—

Jeweler's sand, which is oil based, or green foundry sand, which has water as a binder.

Tools for working the foam model—

Wire, razor blade, alcohol lamp or candle.

Additivies for jewelry design; silver wire, stones, beads, nails, pieces of glass, found objects, pieces of wood and branches, leather, feathers, and many more things.

Paint brush cleaner—

Solvent for removing the residue foam from the cast object. Paint stripper or remover will work.

Old tooth brush

Sieve—

To filter sand over the model. Screen wire will work or a foundry riddle.

Supplies needed for vaporization casting process.

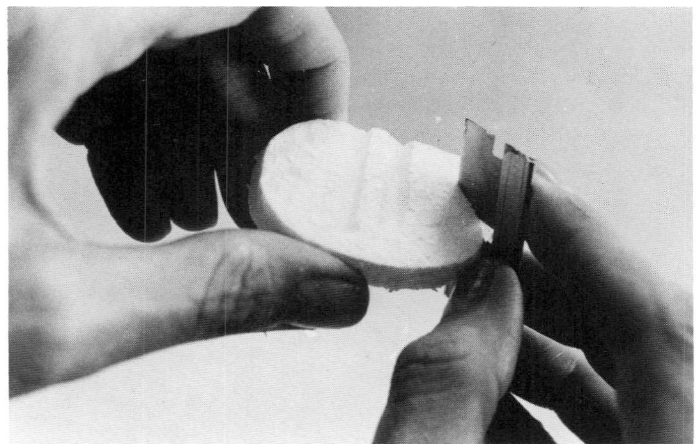

Cut the basic shape and form of the object in polystyrene foam with a single edge razor blade. Surface designs and textures may also be developed with the razor.

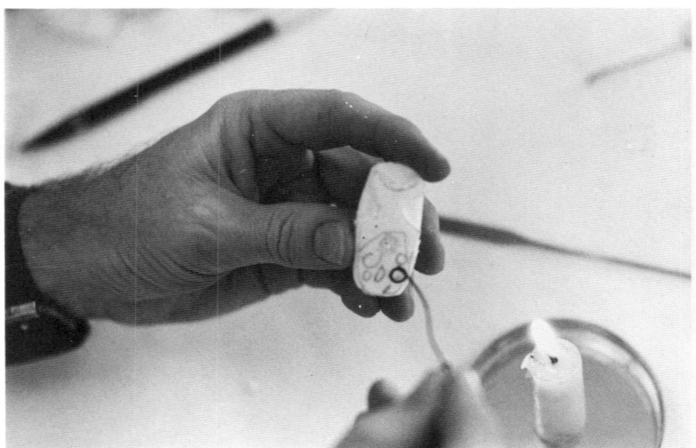

Metal tools and wires bent into desired shapes and heated with a candle, will melt designs into the foam. A hot wire may also be used as a drawing tool.
CAUTION: Have good ventilation

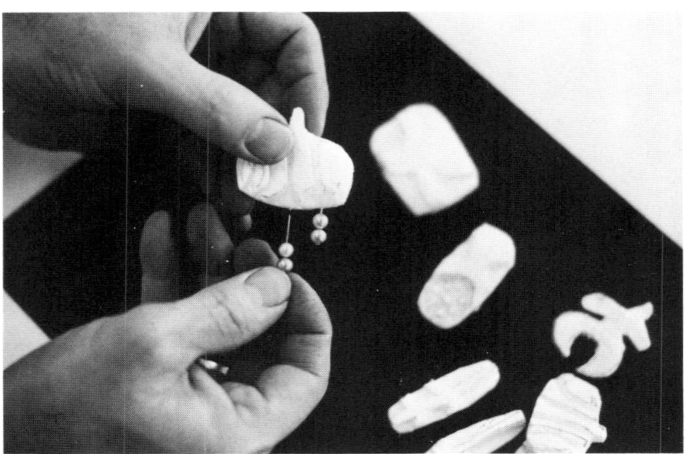

Wire with beads are pushed into the foam.

Foam models ready to be packed in the mold. Additives of all kinds may be added to the design.

Examples of some cast objects with a variety of additives.

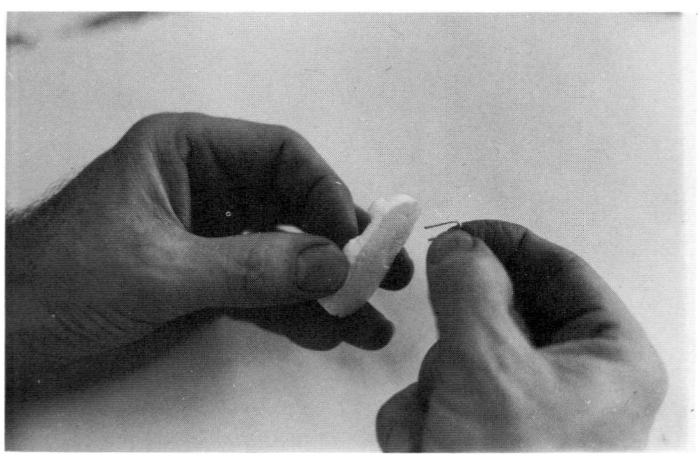

A pendant bail may be inserted in the foam before casting.

The development of the foam model for vaporization casting can be an exciting experience in itself. This unique process allows many variations in constructing jewelry ideas. It should be remembered that the final cast piece will look exactly as the completed matrix, except that pewter will replace the foam.

Two types of sand are available for the casting of pewter by the vaporization technique. The green sand, which may be acquired from local foundries, is a water base casting sand. Water is periodically added to temper the cohesiveness of the sand. To check the moisture content, tightly squeeze a handful of sand. If the shape holds together and, when broken, has clean, sharp edges, the sand is ready for packing. Experimentation will determine the best moisture content for your needs. The second type of casting sand, jeweler's sand or oil base sand, is available through art supply dealers. The oil additive in the sand does not evaporate during use and may be used repeatedly without any special preparation.

Select a can large enough to hold the model without touching the sides. Pack the sand tightly in the bottom one-third of the flask and level it with a piece of wood.

Riddle a thin layer of sand over the packed sand.

Pack sand into the surface detail of the foam model and carefully place it in the loose sand in the bottom of the flask, face down.

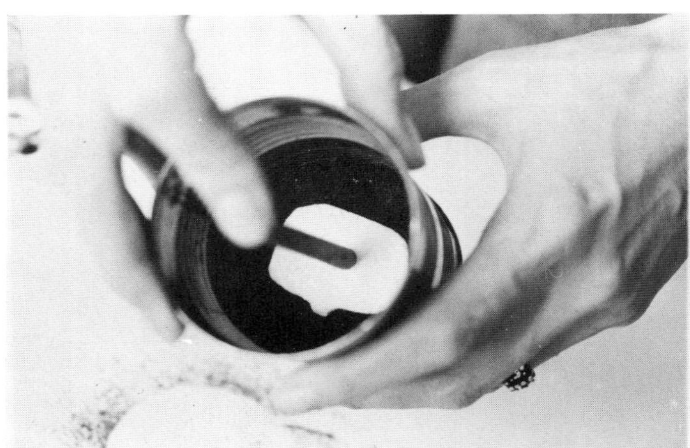

Hold a dowel rod in place against the back of the foam model. When removed, the metal will flow through this passage.

While holding the dowel in place, sift sand around and over the model. Two or more rods may be used with larger pieces to facilitate the flow of metal. Using your fingers, pack the sand firmly in the mold.

Form a cup in the sand with the lowest point next to the dowel. Invert the flask and remove the sprue pin with a twisting motion. After the pin is removed, pack loose sand around the sprue hole, and make sure you can see the white foam at the bottom of the sprue.

Place the flask in the casting area and charge the molten pewter directly into the sprue hole and onto the foam. Heat the pewter a few minutes longer to insure a high temperature in order to complete the vaporization of the foam.

After the pewter has solidified, remove the casting by squeezing the flask. Remove the sand on the casting with a toothbrush. Soak the cast jewelry piece in paint remover or brush cleaner and brush the casting to remove residue styrene. Then finish as suggested. Good ventilation should be provided for safety precautions.

Nine pendants. Author.

Pendant with walnut, vaporization casting. Author.

Foam model. Walnut and appliqued form.

Finished pendant with walnut. Student.

Three pendants, rosewood inlay, encased stone and Herkimer diamond. Author.

Four pendants. Student and the author.

Pendant with sodalite. Wire prongs were cast in the mold. Glass or stones may be set by pushing them into the foam and covering with tissue paper. Student.

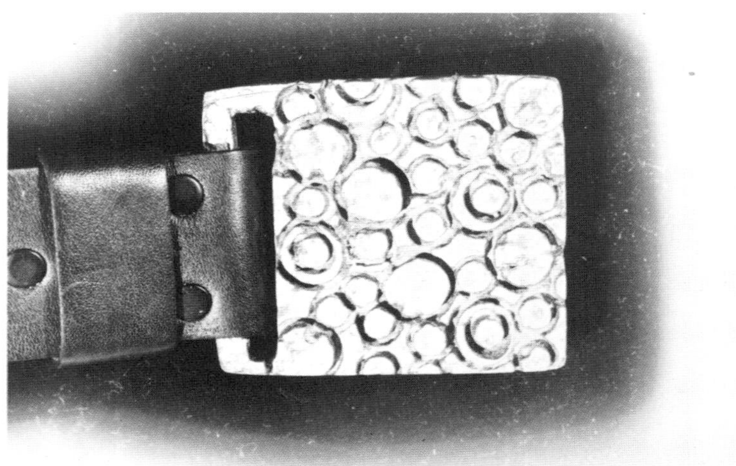

Belt buckle. Design was developed with a hot wire. Student.

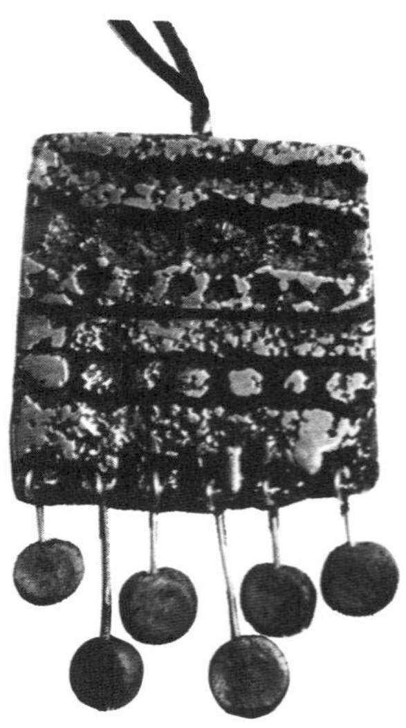

Pendant with clay beads. Student.

Pendant. Author.

Pendant with turquoise beads. Author.

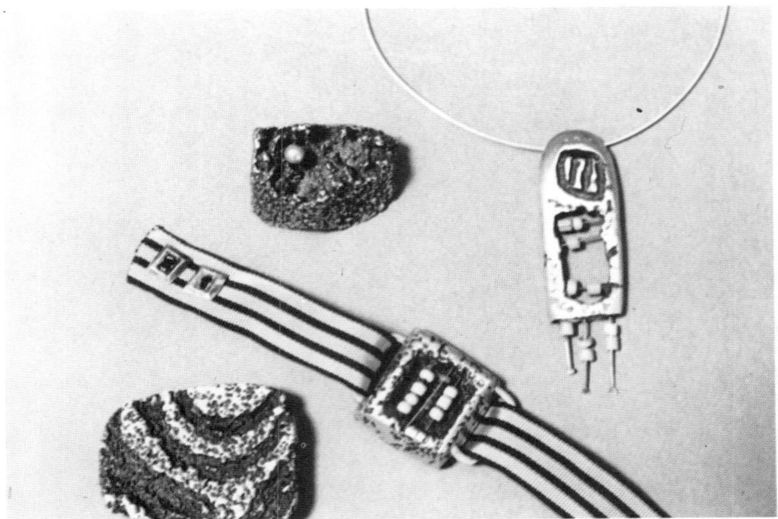
Pins, bracelet, and pendant. Student.

Sand Mold

Sand casting is an excellent process for casting simple jewelry pieces using a rigid model which may be reused many times. A simple description of the basic process is to make a model of the desired piece from a rigid material and place it on a flat surface with a frame around it. Pack jewelers' sand firmly around the model and frame until the sand becomes self-supporting, invert the frame and remove the model carefully. A sprue block is secured to the sand mold and molten pewter is charged into the impression which will produce a metal object the exact shape of the model.

The basic process of sand mold casting requires the suggested items, most of which are available from art supply sources, local industry and school metal shops.

Cope frame (without pins) — wood boxes or tin cans with one or both ends open.
Drag frame (with pins) — necessary only for the split model technique.
Frame boards — Masonite or plywood, large enough to cover cope and drag.
Jewelers' sand — oil base fine sand or may use a water tempered foundry sand.
Parting powder — only for split model, talcum or body powder will work.
Brush and soda straw — for cleaning out sand cavity.
Models — balsa wood, cardboard, soap, plastic or metal.
Sealer for models — diluted white glue, matt medium, shellac, plastic spray.
Steel wool — to polish model after sealer.

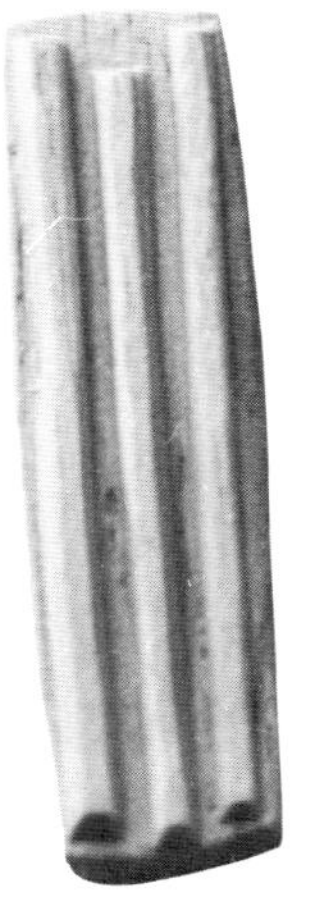

Models ready to be packed in sand. L; appliqued balsa wood, R; carved wood model. Make models from any rigid material.

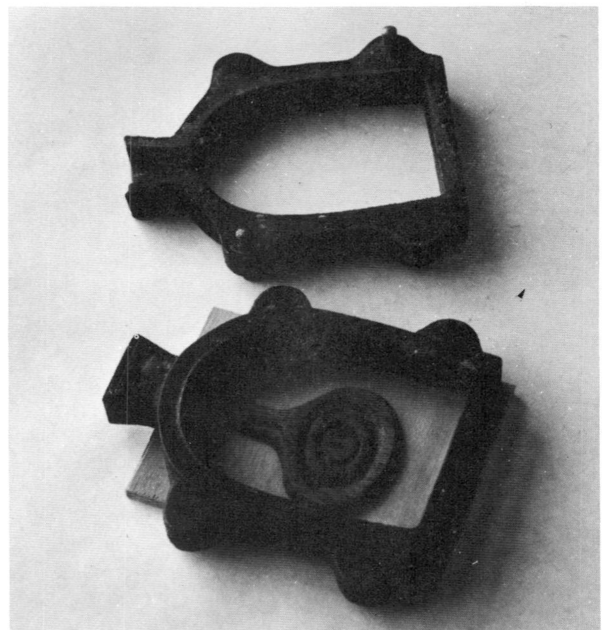

Place wood model on the back board inside the cope.

Sprinkle jewelry sand over model.

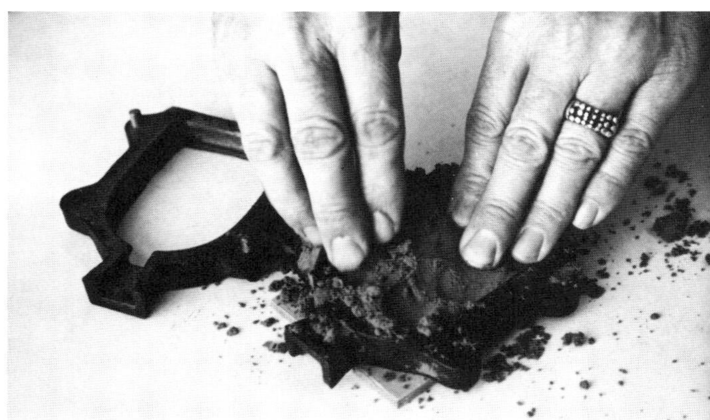

Press the sand firmly into the mold with fingers.

Scrape the excess sand from the cope and place board over the cope. Hold the two boards firmly and turn the mold over. Remove the back board to expose the model.

Lift the model out carefully leaving the impression in the sand.

Use a soft brush or blow excess sand out of mold with a soda straw.

Clamp mold, back board and sprue block together and charge with pewter.

Finished pendant cast in a sand mold.

Pendant and balsa wood model. Student.

Pendant from balsa wood model. Student.

Pendant from balsa wood model. Student.

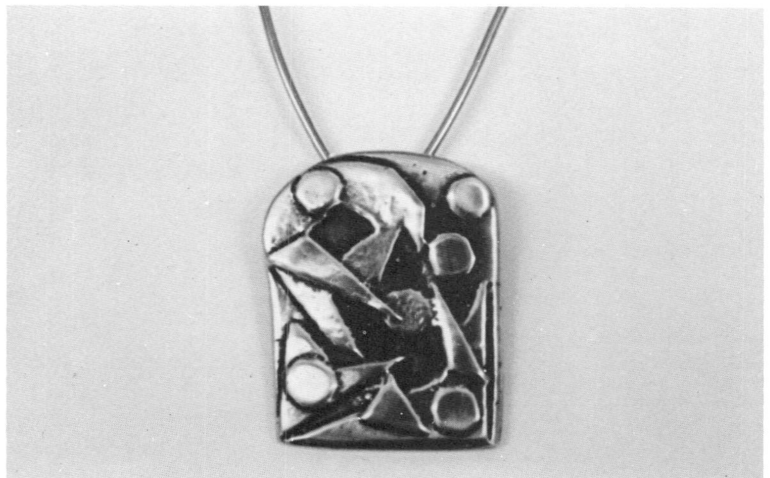

Pendant from cardboard model. Student.

Belt buckles from cardboard model. High school student.

Two-piece balsa wood model with alignment pins and holes.

Place the model with holes face up on the back board with cope in position. Sprinkle sand over the model and press firmly with the fingers. The excess sand is leveled off with a flat surface.

Place the back board on the top of the sand and turn the mold over. Align the pins of the second half of the model with the holes of the first half.

Dust parting powder (or baby powder) over the entire surface. This prevents the sand from sticking together when packing the drag. Brush off excess powder on the model to insure an accurate reproduction.

Place the drag, with pins, on the cope.

Sprinkle sand over the model in the drag.

After the sand is rammed and leveled, carefully separate the cope and drag, exposing the two half models.

Carefully remove the two half models, avoid breaking the sand mold.

Cut a sprue in the sand leading from the opening to the model cavity.

Clamp the cope, drag two back boards together and charge with pewter.

Separate the mold exposing the pewter filled cavity.

Remove the jewelry sand from the casting with a toothbrush.

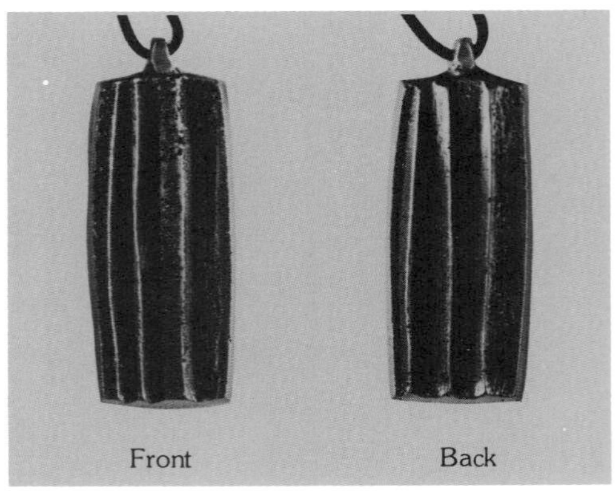

Front Back

The finished cast piece.

Create a casting design in the sand-packed cope with any improvised tool. Pack the sand firmly in the design area and carve a sprue in the sand or use a wood sprue block.

Wood, stones or other objects may also be placed in the cavity of the mold.

The wood and pewter casting after removal from the mold.

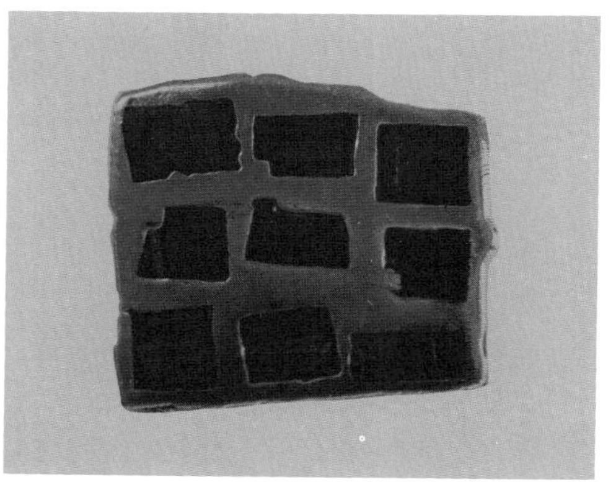

The finished pin, walnut. Student.

Use a cardboard model to develop a uniform shape and then stamp or carve textures in the sand mold.

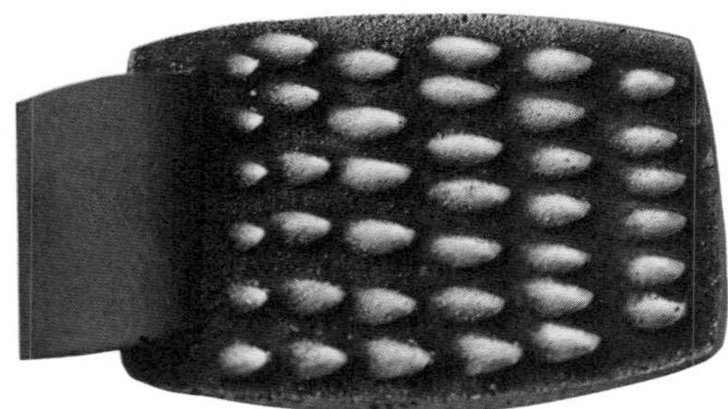

A belt buckle.

Pendant with stamped textures. Student.

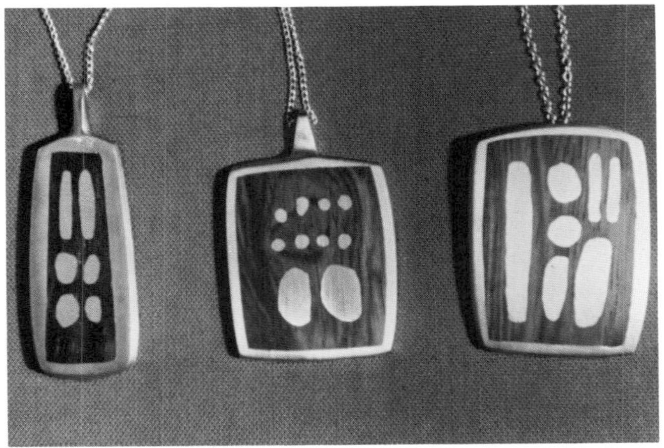

Three pendants, rosewood, sand mold casting. Author.

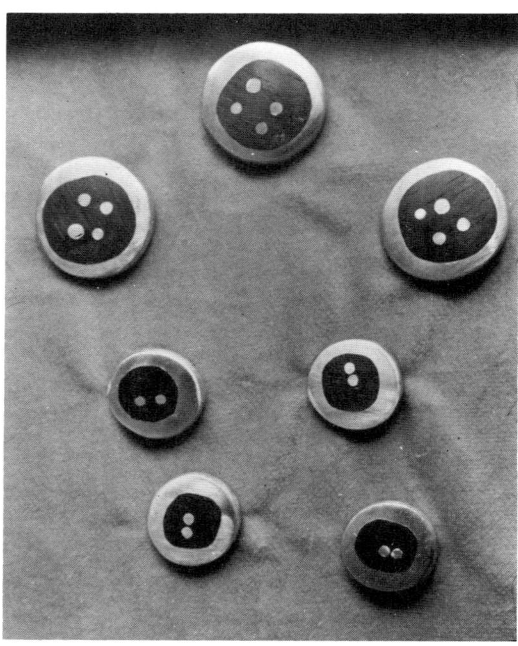

Buttons for a coat, rosewood, sand mold casting. Author.

Pendants and pin, rosewood and ebony. Student.

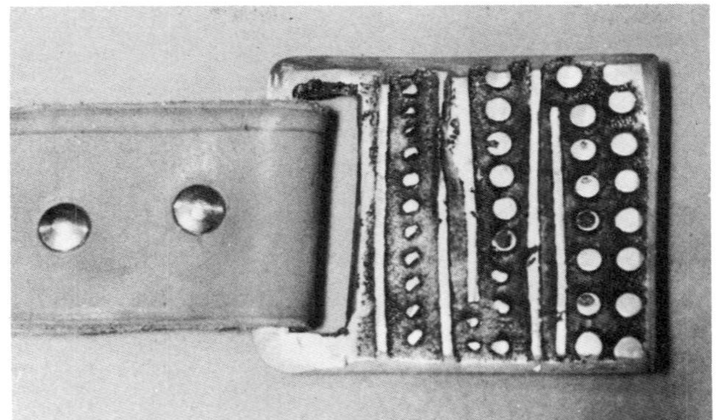

Belt buckle. Student.

Pendant. Rosewood, ebony, walnut. Author.

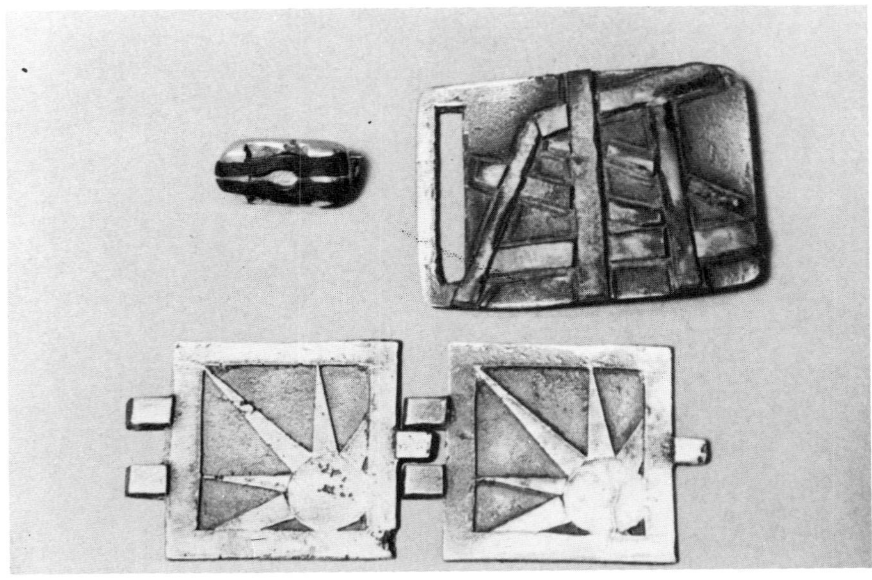

Buckle and pin. High school student.

Pendant. Ebony. Author.

Buttons, macramé watch bands. Author and Jean L. Kain.

Aluminum Foil Mold

Aluminum foil, which melts at approximately 1200°F, makes an excellent mold material for the low melting temperature of pewter. Three different gauges of foil are available for use as casting molds. The household aluminum foil is available in all food stores in regular and heavy duty weights. These foils can be used in single or double layers for added strength and durability of the mold. Repoussé foil, available from art suppliers in 36 gauge weight, may be used as the mold for casting pewter.

Create interesting surface textures by wrinkling the aluminum foil. Fold the edges of the foil to construct a reservoir for the metal. Walls should not be too high as they determine the thickness and weight of the casting.

Burnish the inside of the aluminum box to create the surface design. Wood, plastic or metal tools may be used.

Place the aluminum mold in a pit or container of sand and charge molten pewter into the open mold.

Immediately press a block of wood or plaster down gently on top of the molten pewter forcing the excess metal out of the mold. This will reduce the thickness and weight of the jewelry piece.

The overflow areas of pewter are easily broken off with a pair of pliers. Brush the waste pewter clean of the sand and reuse it for other casting. After the metal cools, gently peel the foil off and finish the pewter piece.

Many objects may be included in the aluminum mold to be cast permanently in the pewter. Example, old nails pushed through the walls of the foil.

Rosewood slipped into slots in the foil mold.

Nails inserted in the front of the mold. The inserted ends of the nails will be covered and secured in pewter.

Secure stones by squeezing the foil around part of it or by gluing the stone to the foil.

Aluminum foil partially removed from the cast pewter piece with a stone.

Finished pendant with agate.

Six wires placed in the mold to set a cabochon stone. After the piece is cast, the stone will be placed and the wires chased around it. Achieve patterns and repetitions in the foil mold by rubbing over surfaces with unique textures. Example, a hair comb texture was used.

Finished pin with Jasper Canyon agate. Author.

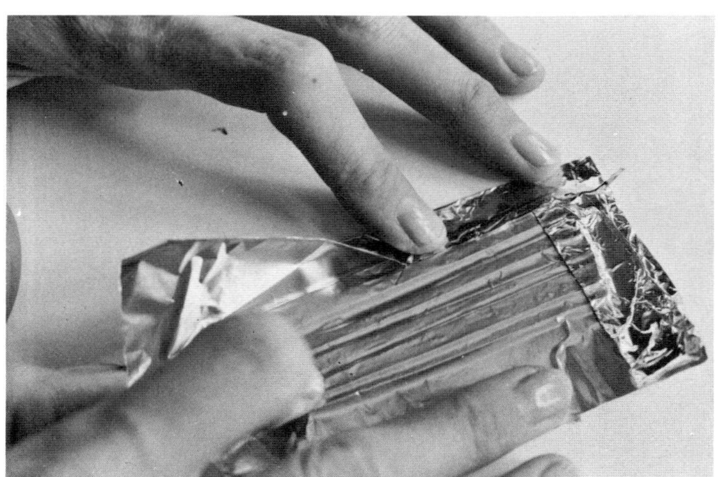

Burnish or rub the foil over the cardboard models to achieve the same impression of design. Double-over the edges of the foil to add strength to the mold.

The depth of the mold depends on the thickness of the cardboard. By not gluing down the raised shapes more spontaneity may be achieved from the models. This mold is ready to charge.

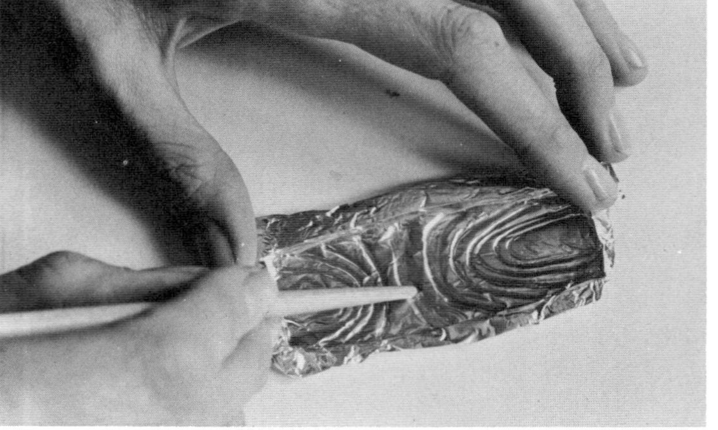

Model the foil over the basic cardboard shape and then burnish the surface for added designs.

Cardboard model and string will create interesting designs.

White glue squeezed onto model and left to dry will create interesting textures and designs.

Finished pendant with dried glue texture.

Pins and pendants, cardboard and string technique.

Pendants, wrinkled foil technique. Jean L. Kain.

Bracelet with pearl, aluminum foil mold. Jean L. Kain.

Pendant, silver wire and walnut, wrinkled and sand texture. Author.

Pendant, burnished technique. Silver wire, rosewood and pheasant feathers. Author.

Pendants, L. burnished technique, R. rubbing over a feather. Student.

Pendant, Foil burnished over screen wire. Student.

Pendant, lace agate, silver wire and rosewood. Jean L. Kain.

Two pendants. Pecos diamond, rosewood. Author.

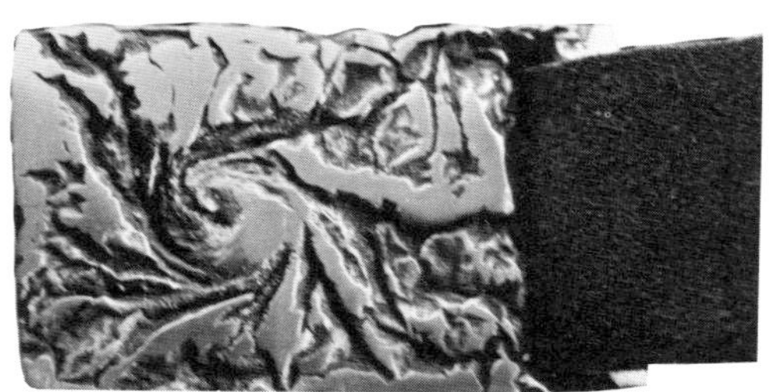

Belt buckle. Adult student.

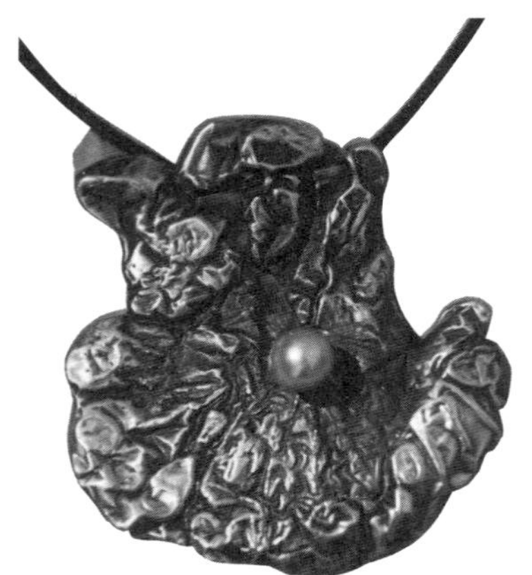

Pendant with baroque pearl, aluminum foil mold. Author.

Pendants with antique nails.

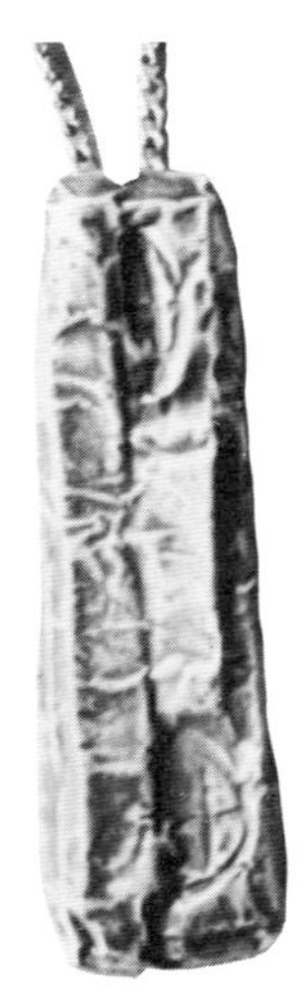
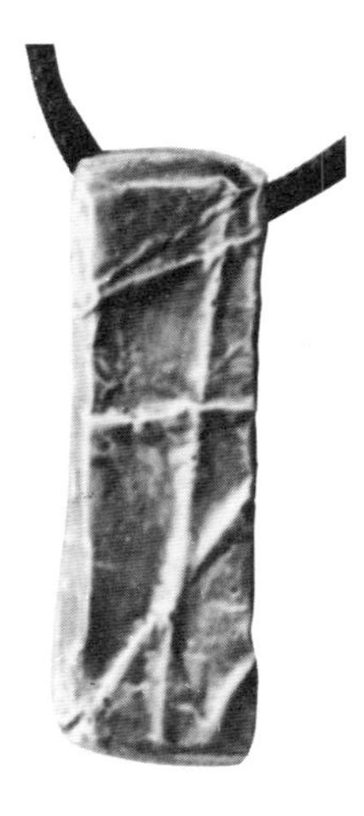

Two pendants. Brad Kain, age 10.

Pendant. Jaye Kain, age 13.

Water Pour

Pouring molten metal into a can of water will produce a variety of shapes and forms which could be identified by the artist as possible pieces for jewelry. These pieces could be used independently, as a module unit, or mounted on other materials such as wood or leather.

A tall can, with a low water level, is best used as the receptacle for the molten pewter pour. The high sides of the can will help restrict the splashing of the water or metal. The temperature of the water will vary the effects of the shapes, as will the temperature of the pewter during the charging. A quantity of pewter should be charged in short pours to provide a good selection of shapes from which to choose. It is next to impossible to pre-determine the exact shape.

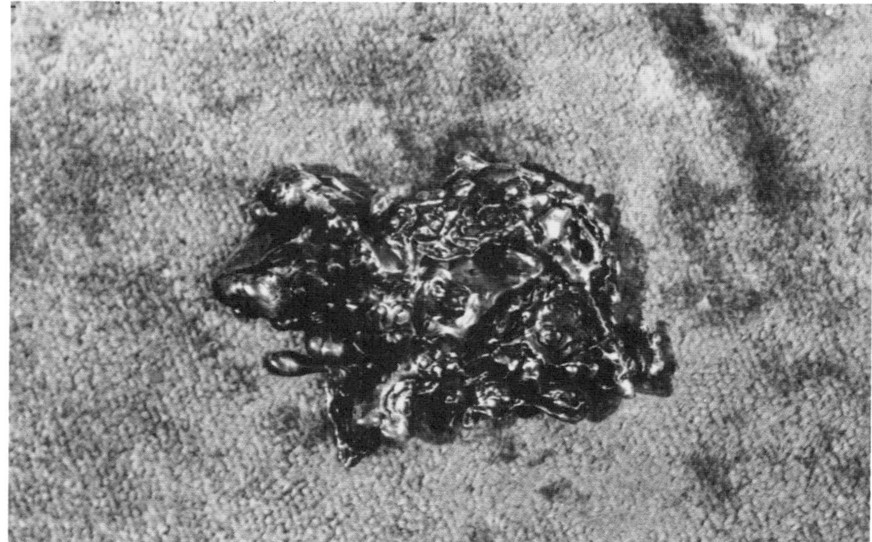

Pin, molten pewter poured into a container of water. Student.

Pendant, water pour. Student.

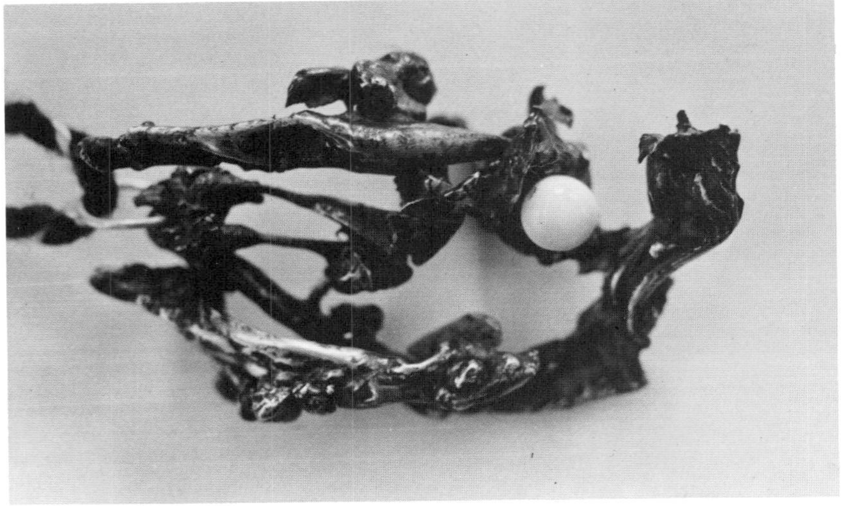
Pendant with bead, water pour technique. Student.

Random Pour

Molten pewter may be poured or splashed onto an asbestos sheet, refractory bricks or wood to produce purely accidental happenings and unique shapes. From these shapes additional designs may be introduced by sawing, texturing or remelting parts of the cast pewter. Extreme caution should be taken to safeguard against the metal splashing onto clothes or skin.

Pendants. Molten pewter is poured onto a sheet of asbestos, causing bubbles. The negative areas were removed by sawing. Student.

FINISHING PROCEDURES

IV

Filing & Surface Treatment

After the pewter object has been cast and taken from the mold, the final step is to file and polish the rough casting and to secure any necessary jewelry findings. This is an important step in determining the final appearance of the cast object as it may either retain its original textures and shape; or, by extensive filing or cutting, the object may be reshaped from the original to create modified forms and textures.

Sprues and unwanted areas of pewter are easily cut off the cast object with a hacksaw, a jeweler's saw or even a pair of tin snips. If the pewter piece has to be placed in the vise, it should be wrapped in paper to protect it from being scratched. Tin snips may also be used to cut off any thin flashes of metal around the cast object.

Tools used for finishing the cast pieces of pewter jewelry, R-L Tin snips, jeweler's saw, hand and needle files, file card for cleaning files, abrasive paper and steel wool.

Filing the soft pewter with metal files will remove the flashes, rough edges, or any other unwanted areas of metal. Since the pewter is very soft, it will clog the files rapidly, so a file brush or card brush should be used often to keep the file teeth clean and free of pewter. It is best to use a specific set of files for the pewter work only, and not use them interchangeably with other metals such as gold or silver.

Different grades of steel wool and abrasive papers are available in local hardware stores. These materials are used to remove the file marks and to polish the surfaces of the cast pewter object.

Surface textures may be achieved with special chasing tools or with any metal object or tool that could be used as a stamp. Metal gravers will cut the soft pewter easily to create line designs in cast pieces, as well as metal scribes or nails which will also scratch lines into the surface for added decorative textures.

Oxidizing

To oxidize the pewter, the object is submerged in a solution of nitric acid and water. The solution is prepared from one part acid to five to seven parts water ALWAYS ADD ACID TO WATER.

The acid solution should be kept in a covered glass container and the container should be properly LABELLED! Good ventilation should also be provided in the working area. Safety precautions should be taken at all times while working around the acid.

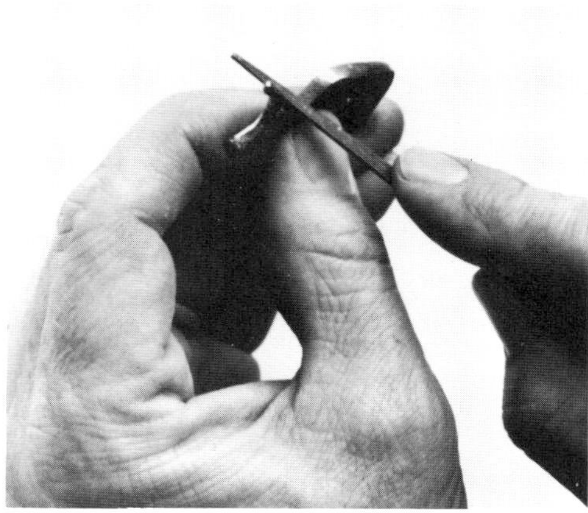

Use hand files to remove rough surfaces and to reshape the object. Use needle files to smooth detailed areas of the casting.

Nitric acid (one part) mixed into water (5 parts) will oxidize pewter. Use a glass container with lid and good ventilation. CAUTION

Use tongs to dip the objects into the acid solution. CAUTION. Rinse the object clean of the excess acid with running water and dry with paper towel.

Polishing

After the piece is oxidized, a fine grade of steel wool (000 or 00) or wet-dry carborundum paper (320 to 600 grit) may be used to remove the oxidization from the raised portions of the surface. This will expose the warmth of the metal and show the contrast between the metal and the oxidization. Generally, this could be the final polishing step if the desired result is a satin finish, or if polishing equipment is not available. A higher polish may be achieved by hand buffing with a tripoli, which is an abrasive, to remove the minute scratches left by the paper or steel wool. To bring the piece to its final luster, polish it with rouge compound. The best way to obtain a high luster is with a machine buffer if one is available. Buffing equipment used for pewter should be restricted for pewter only as the soft metal may contaminate the buffs.

Safety precautions should be followed at all times when using the buffing wheel for polishing. Always use goggles to protect the eyes and don't wear clothing or articles that could be caught or tangled with the buffing wheel. Keep long hair out of the way with a rubber band. Involvement with any power machinery requires the utmost of caution. Always check to make sure that the metal object is securely held or clamped in a ring holder to prevent it from being thrown by the wheel.

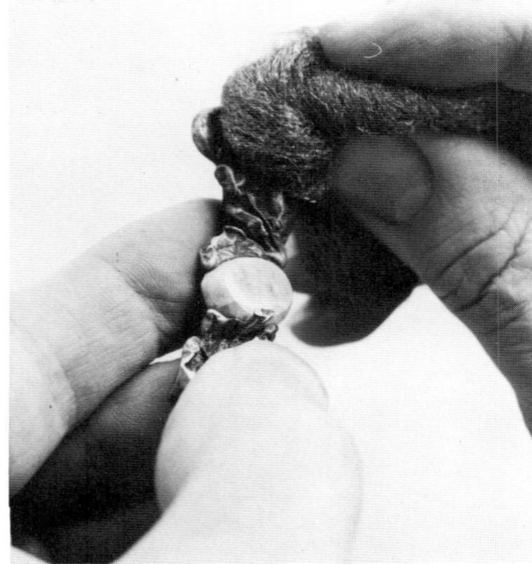

Use abrasive papers, such as emery cloth, crocus paper or carborundum paper (wet and dry) to remove the oxidization from the surface and add a satin polish to the pewter. Fine grades of steel wool will also accomplish this purpose.

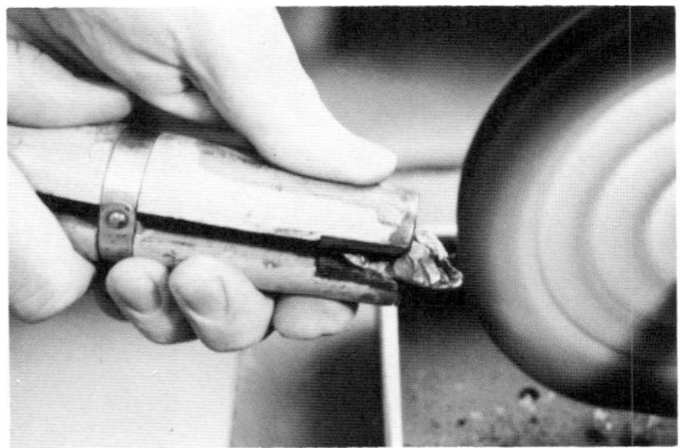

Buff with tripoli, an abrasive, to remove steel wool or paper scratches. Use only the bottom quadrant of the buffer. USE CAUTION.

Rouge will add a high sheen to the pewter. Maintain separate buffs especially for pewter.

Soldering

Soldering pewter is difficult for the beginner because of the small difference between the melting temperature of the pewter and the melting point of the solder. Special pewter solder may be purchased from art supply sources which is approximately 45 parts tin, 27 parts lead and 28 parts bismuth and has flowing temperature of below 300°F. Special flux is recommended for use with this solder. It may be made by combining approximately 10 drops of hydrochloric acid with one ounce of gylcerine. Regular soft soldering paste may be used with satisfactory results.

One procedure for soldering a pin back onto a pewter jewelry piece is to sweat solder (flow solder onto the surface by heating) both the object and the pin back. Place the two pieces together and secure with baling wire or soldering clamps and again flux the joints thoroughly. Solder flows by capillary action, so it is necessary that all parts being soldered must touch each other. Heat slowly and evenly with a torch or an electric soldering gun until the solder flows from between the two pieces. Let the piece cool and then clean it with soap and water.

The back of the pewter casting may be sprayed with lacquer or fixative spray to avoid air oxidization of the metal. Periodic polishing will be necessary to retain the luster of the pewter jewelry.

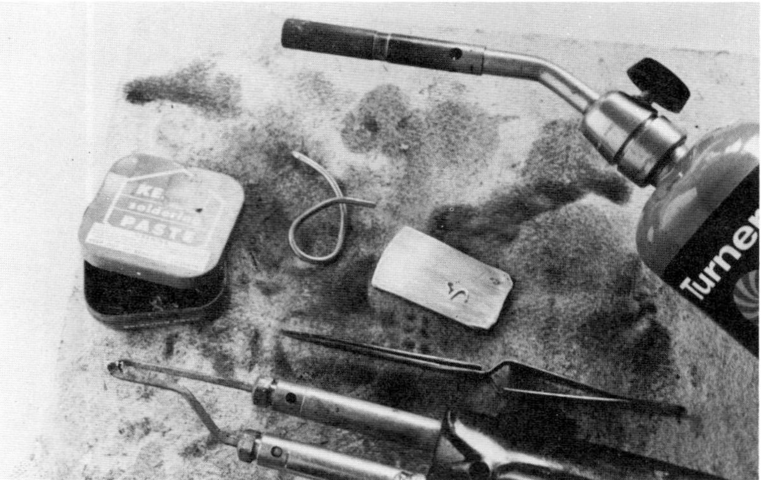

Soldering equipment and supplies: Soldering flux, pewter solder, soldering tongs, torch or electric gun and asbestos sheet.

Apply soldering flux to the immediate area of the two metals to be joined and place small paillons of solder beside the joints of the bail and piece. With the soldering tweezers holding the pendant bail, slowly apply heat with the torch. USE CAUTION or the pewter will melt.

Soldering with an electric gun.

Wash the back of the object with soap and water and polish with steel wool.

To keep the pewter from oxidizing, spray a coating of krylon on the back of the object.

APPENDIX

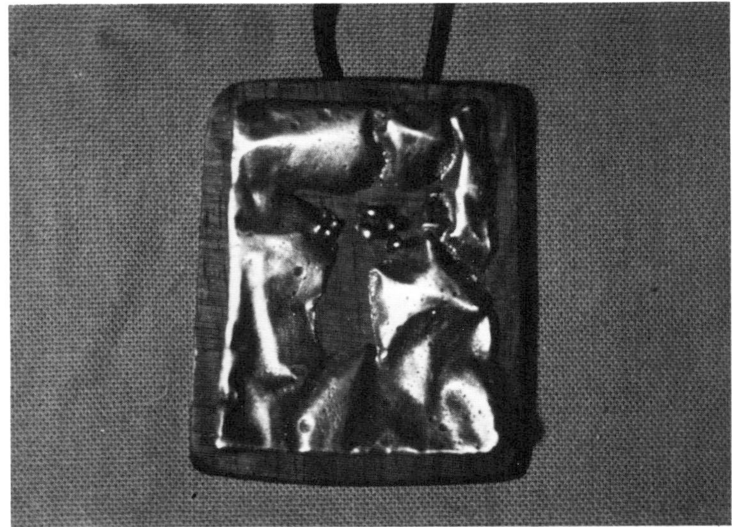

Pendant with rosewood, aluminum foil mold. Jean L. Kain.

Belt Buckle, plaster block casting. Student.

BIBLIOGRAPHY

Bovin, Murray. JEWELRY MAKING. Murray Bovin Publisher. Forest Hills, N.Y. 16th printing 1972.

_______________ JEWELRY CASTING. Murray Bovin Publisher. Forest Hills, N.Y. 1971.

Choate, Sharr. CREATIVE CASTING. Crown Publishing, Inc. New York N.Y. 1966.

Cotterell, Howard Herschel; Riff Adolphe; Vetter, Robert M. NATIONAL TYPES OF OLD PEWTER. The Pyne Press. Princeton, N.J. Copyright 1972 revised by the Magazine ANTIQUES.

Crawford, John. INTRODUCING JEWELRY MAKING. Watson-Guptill Publications. New York, N.Y. 1969.

Feirer, John L. GENERAL METALS. McGraw-Hill Book Company. New York, N.Y. 1959 Second Edition.

Franke, Lois E. HANDWROUGHT JEWELRY. McKnight and McKnight Publishing Co. Bloomington, Ill. 1962.

Gentille, Thomas. STEP-BY-STEP JEWELRY. Golden Press. New York, N.Y. 1968.

Grando, Michael D. JEWELRY-FORM AND TECHNIQUE. Van Nostrand Reinhold Co. New York, N.Y. 1969.

Kauffman, Henry J. THE AMERICAN PEWTERER. Thomas Nelson, Inc. Camden, N.J. 1970.

Kerfoot, J.B. AMERICAN PEWTER. Bonanza Books. New York, N.Y. 1924.

Morton, Philip. CONTEMPORARY JEWELRY. A Studio Handbook. Holt, Rinehart and Winston, Inc. New York, N.Y. 1969.

Untracht, Oppi. METAL TECHNIQUES FOR CRAFTSMEN. Doubleday and Company, Inc. Garden City, N.Y. 1968.

Wholrabe, Raymond A. METALS. Lippincott Company. New York, N.Y. 1964.

Willcox, Donald J. NEW DESIGN IN JEWELRY. Van Nostrand Reinhold Company. New York, N.Y. 1970.

GLOSSARY

Abrasive Paper	Emery cloth, crocus paper, carborundum paper—a coated abrasive on paper used to remove file marks and scratches on metal.
Alloy	A composition of two or more metals.
Aluminum foil	Commercial household foil and heavy duty foil may be purchased at super markets. 36 gauge foil may be acquired from art supply sources.
Bezel	The thin band of metal that is used to secure cabochon stones to metal jewelry. May be cast in the metal piece or soldered on after casting.
Burnout Kilns	Small oven or heating chamber that will heat flask and melt the wax model. Should reach temperatures of 1000 to 1100 degrees F.
Casting Pit	A container filled with sand or dirt in which the mold is placed for casting.
Charge	The action of pouring the molten metal into the mold.
Chase	To push back or in, to make impressions from the front of sheet metal.
Cope and Drag	Two similar wood or metal frames used in sand casting. Cope has holes and the drag has pins (lugs) for alignment of the two flasks.
Debubblizer	A commercial substance that is applied over the wax model to help the liquid investment obtain a smooth surface and to prohibit air bubbles. Liquid green soap will work.
Ductile	Refers to metals that are capable of being drawn into fine wire.
Filigree	Fine wires, lacy and delicate jewelry.
Fissure	Openings between the block molds or cracks in the investment molds.
Flashes, Metal	Metal that flows into the fissures between the molds. Easily removed and finished.
Flask	A metal ring open on one or both ends used to hold investment for lost wax casting. Tin can which is open on one end used to hold sand for vaporization. Cope and drag frames used for sand casting.
Flux	Liquid or paste substance which prevents oxidation of metal when heated and it also aids the flow of solder.

Gravity Casting Casting without assistance of pressure, vacuum or centrifuge. The weight of the metal (specific gravity) is the only force which is used to make the metal impression.

Jeweler's Sand A fine grade sand mixed with an oil binder used as a mold material for casting. Acquired from art supply sources.

Ladle A container with a handle for melting and pouring the molten pewter. Clay, cast iron, copper or an old soup ladle spoon will work.

Malleable Refers to metals capable of being stretched or harden without cracking or breaking.

Model A pattern of the exact piece of jewelry to be cast. Wax models for lost wax process, balsa and cardboard models for sand casting process and foam models for vaporization casting process.

Moulding Plaster A calcined gypsum similar to plaster of paris. May be purchased from local hardware, building supplies stores.

Nitric Acid $HN0_3$ Used to oxidize pewter. 1 part nitric acid mixed into 5 parts water.

Pewter An alloy of approximate 90% tin, 8% antimony and 2% copper. Melts at approximately 450 degrees F. to 500 degrees F.

Pewter Solder Bismuth or pewter solder is 28% bismuth, 45% tin and 27% lead will melt and flow at 300°F. Soft commercial solder of 60% tin, 40% lead melts at 340°F will work with pewter.

Polystyrene Foam Expanded liquid polystyrene of Dow Chemical Co. is trademarked "Styrofoam". Expanded beads of polystyrene can be found as packing material.

Repoussé To push metal forward, to make raised areas in sheet metal by working from the back side of the sheet.

Riser A large funnel or passage way in the investment which allows the molten metal to flow up after filling the mold cavity.

Rouge A fine polishing compound for metal.

Slag The impurities in the metal which rise to the surface during the melting process.

Solidify The hardening of the molten metal as it cools or freezes.

Sprue The opening through which molten metal is poured into the mold.

Sprue Block Wooden or plaster block that has a carved out passeway for the molten metal to flow through to the cavity in the design block.

Sweat Soldering (or tinning) A method of flowing solder onto the area of each piece to be soldered together and then placing the two pieces together and reheating to secure.

Tripoli A fast cutting abrasive for removing scratches from metal.

Vaporization Casting Also called full mold. Investment or foundry sand is placed around foam model. The foam model remains in the mold during the charging as the molten pewter melts the foam to replace it.

Vents Small passages scratched in plaster mold blocks for release of gases. In the lost-wax process the vents are made of wax wires which melt during burn-out.

SOURCES FOR LEAD-FREE PEWTER

Allcraft Tool and Supply Co., Inc.
215 Park Ave.
Hicksville, NY 11801

T. E. Conklin Brass and Copper Co., Inc.
324 West 23rd St.
New York, NY

El Dorado Sales
P.O. Box 1451
Bellevue, Washington 98009

T. B. Hagstoz and Son
709 Sansom Street
Philadelphia, PA 19106

Ney Smelting and Refining Co. Inc.
269 Freeman Street
Brooklyn, NY 11222

White Metal Rolling and Stamping Corp.
80 Moultrie Street
Brooklyn, NY 11222

Sax Arts and Crafts
207 North Milwaukee Street
Milwaukee, Wisconsin 53202

C. R. Hill Co.
2734 W. 11 Hile Rd.
Berkley, Michigan 48072